GOD DOES N̶O̶T̶ EXIST

One Man's Journey from Hell to

Heaven and Back

By

Joseph C Hirl

Library of Congress Cataloging-in-Publication Data is available.

978-1-7321581-0-8	Kindle/AZW
978-1-7321581-1-5	Epub
978-1-7321581-2-2	Mobi
978-1-7321581-3-9	PDF
978-1-7321581-4-6	Paperback
978-1-7321581-5-3	Hardcover

This book is a memoir. It reflects the author's present recollections of experiences over time. This is a work of nonfiction. No names have been changed, no characters invented, no events fabricated and some dialogue has been recreated.

Cover Design by Joseph C Hirl.

Book design by Rasel Khondokar.

Printed by Joseph Hirl, in the United States of America.

First printing edition 2018.

Joseph Hirl

PO BOX 1021

Big Rapids, MI 49307

www.joeyhirl.com

Dedication

Dedicated to the ones who are suffering, to the ones
who believe and the ones that don't yet believe
because, in the end, we are all believers.

Table of Contents

Preface

I was a poor kid that grew up with nothing in the roughest parts of Boston. No money, no faith and no hope. My childhood was one full of pain, abuse and darkness... Abandoned by my father at a young age and left with an abusive mother. All I had were my siblings Jimmy, Denise and Cindi. As a young adult, I was always hustling, breaking the law and a real hard ass. I was cocky and with a chip on my shoulder a mile wide. I got in trouble, paid my dues. Got myself straight – I took a chance and started a successful painting business from scratch, with no help from anyone and 100 dollars in my pocket. I got married, had kids of my own. I left my childhood and all the bad memories behind. I was good at leaving things behind, especially things that made me feel bad or reminded me of my childhood. My life was good. I made my life the way it was. The only faith I had was in me, there was no God. I was not a believer. Because how could God stand by and let what had happened to my siblings and I when we were kids happen? How?

Then one stormy July night- Pain, darkness, nothing, I died. Dead, my ticket was punched. For 57 minutes, I was clinically dead. It's medically unheard of to come back after that long. I am a true fucking miracle in every sense. Everything I thought I knew or believed in was challenged and pushed beyond the limits of what I thought possible. My world completely shifted from what I knew, to what I could never have imagined. I was 48 years old, my life was over, or so it seemed because when I came back, I was literally reborn. Everything changed, my outlook, my faith, everything. To fully understand what happened that night, you need to understand where I came from. What hell I survived.

CHAPTER 1

God Does Not Exist

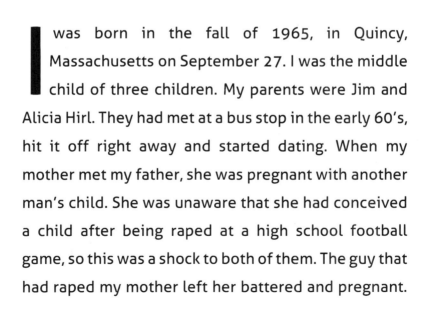

I was born in the fall of 1965, in Quincy, Massachusetts on September 27. I was the middle child of three children. My parents were Jim and Alicia Hirl. They had met at a bus stop in the early 60's, hit it off right away and started dating. When my mother met my father, she was pregnant with another man's child. She was unaware that she had conceived a child after being raped at a high school football game, so this was a shock to both of them. The guy that had raped my mother left her battered and pregnant.

3

My dad saw past this and wanted to raise the baby as his own. However, my father was young too and was not ready to raise a child, especially a child that was a product of a traumatic event. I think he thought he was doing the right thing. My grandmother also wanted my mother to keep the baby. It was the early 1960s and abortion was socially unacceptable and it was against her religious beliefs, being a Catholic and coming from an Irish family, it was not an option. With all the outside influences from family/friends and my father, I can only imagine the pain and suffering my mother had to endure over the rape and the child she was now carrying as a product of that rape. So my mother gave birth to a healthy baby girl and gave her up for adoption that same day. Problem solved, right? I just don't think she was ready to handle a kid yet. Especially a kid that was forced upon her during a violent rape. I believe, at the time, my mother did the right thing. I can only imagine how hard her decisions were to make. To be so young, to be assaulted like that and then have your choices taken away. Not having any power over your body or what happens to you, must have affected her in the worst possible way. It must have been so difficult to act like you were ok with a situation that you had no control over. I think this traumatic situation changed something in her, because she lost control over her own body and life, from that point forward she could never get attached to anyone. Somehow, she found a way of getting back something she had lost that night on the football field; she regained control of her life. She did this through her relationships with men. She was always the one in charge and they never lasted, "hit and runs" they were called.

This was our family's deep dark secret. We would not find out about our sister until we were adults. For many years, my sister Cindi and I tried to find her. We posted information on all of the websites that reunited adoptive kids with their long lost families. The search went on for years with so many disappointments and false leads. When we finally found her, she chose not to have anything to do with us. We received a letter letting us know that she wanted no contact. Maybe she had some animosity against the family that gave her up and left her abandoned. I just do not know. I guess the feeling of being rejected must have hurt her at first, because in your head you imagine how the meeting would go, you just found your long lost sister and then, poof, she's gone once again. I often think to myself how lucky she was; she missed out on being an abused child and growing up in poverty. Sometimes I kind of wished I had been given up for adoption too. I wondered if she had a good life? I wondered if she had a nice house? Maybe two parents? Maybe she got what she asked for at Christmas time, not what was left at the stores or open box toys that were donated to a secret Santa? Maybe she wore new clothes instead of hand me downs or clothes form the Goodwill. I pray she had a good life and did well. After all, she was my older sister.

I guess my first real memories of growing up are in Dorchester, a very poor part of Boston,

Massachusetts. You couldn't find a more perfect breeding ground for abuse and neglect. Poverty stricken buildings, derelict kids running wild, drugs were everywhere; it was the picture of an inner-city ghetto. Do not get me wrong, it was not all bad, the people of DOT, that's what they called themselves, short for Dorchester, took pride in where they lived and where they were raised. It's like you were loyal to the city you were born in and Bostonians are very proud people and take pride in their city, even if some parts of the city is a shit hole. Pride isn't something that can be bought, you have it or you don't. Boston is a very beautiful city, filled with history, beautiful buildings and most of all, beautiful people. Not to mention some of the best sports teams around, GO PATS. The people of Boston are friendly and always seem willing to help you out. But just like any other big city there is the dark side, the drug abuse and crime exist. So, when I say ghetto, I say it with pride and from the heart. I say it like a Bostonian, "A Wicked Pissah Place".

Like any big city, some of the outskirts are downright scary and that is where low-income people lived. Amongst the dope houses, pimps, prostitutes and thieves. Growing up poor creates a community all its own. When you grow up poor, you have to count on more people to survive, whether it was another poor family to split the rent with, a family friend to help pay the bills, neighbors helping one another out, the government for handouts or going to the local drug dealer for a loan until the welfare check comes in. Being poor has its codes to live by. See, when most people run out of money, they go to the bank to get a loan, but when you are poor, you don't have that option. You go see the wise guys or your local drug dealer for a loan. They are tougher than any bank I ever had to deal with. See, no one talks about good credit in the hood, because it does not exist, poor people don't have any credit. What credit they do have is tarnished with missing or late payments. Food stamps were always considered currency in the ghetto and there was always someone willing to pay

50 cents on the dollar for them. Just a plain tough neighborhood to live in and even tougher place to grow up in.

When I was four, my father left behind my mother and the three of us children; Jimmy, my sister Cindi and myself. My parents were young at the time and they always seemed to be fighting and just could never get it together. They were two opposites trying to make it work out and raise a family. I remember their last fight. It was on a cold and snowy night. They were fighting like they always did and the next day he was gone. I remember looking for him out the window through the snow, wondering when he was going to return. He never did and I blamed myself for that. And so did my mother or at least it felt that way to me. He was not what a father should be. His evil surfaced later in life when my sister told me my father had sexually assaulted her at a young age. Did we really want or need him in our lives? Yeah, my father was a horrible monster and my mother would always let me know just how horrible he was and how much I reminded her of him. My father did a lot of fucked up things. He definitely was not a role model by any stretch of the imagination, maybe the farthest thing from a role model or a father. We had no support from my father, he was a deadbeat dad, and I guess if you looked in the dictionary under deadbeat dads, you would see a picture of him. He owed our family hundreds of thousands in child support and never paid a penny. He always had an angle for getting money and just getting by. I guess he never held a job for too long, his drug habit was his full time job. Chasing drugs, speed (diet pills) ruled his life. Taking speeders, you think he would have had the energy to work a full time job, but it seemed chasing drugs kept him too busy to work. I remember he had a job for a short time at a packy. A packy is where you buy your booze and beer. While he was working we would stop by and he would give us each a Slim Jim when we were hungry, you can't live off of Slim Jims and I remembered still being hungry after my Slim Jim was gone. We had two parents that were monsters. Did we even have a fighting chance from the get go to survive, I doubt it.

My mother was very abusive (abusive is putting it so lightly, she was downright mean as hell) and it was always directed at me, she would always say, "you look like your dad" while beating my ass, and "You will never amount to anything". The ass beatings were easy to swallow, don't get me wrong, they hurt like hell, but the pain of her verbal cruelty was beyond any physical wounds. It always cut deep and scarred me for years to come. Little did I know it would affect my whole life, then and now. My mother was verbally abusive to everyone she met, my father, her many boyfriends and family. Nothing or no one was off limits, absolutely nothing. My mother was a very angry and volatile person.

I remember my mother saying mean things to me like "The best part of you ran down your father's leg, I should have swallowed you, I should have aborted you, and you will never amount to nothing, just like your father". How do you tell a young kid that? How do you damage a young mind like that? Over time, you begin to believe what your mother tells you every day. As a parent, how do you look at yourself in the mirror after saying such things to your kid? This was the time that she should have been laying down the fundamentals of what it meant to be a good child, how to become a good person. The ground rules for life, like there are consequences for your actions. Rules that are such common sense, like treat others how you want to be treated, don't lie, and don't be cruel. Such as the things you say and do to others can hurt them. These values should have been instilled in me when I was young and carried me into my adulthood. The same values I would later instill in my children. Instead, she was damaging me, plucking away everything that made me human, she plucked out every bit of humanity that I had in me, piece by piece. Leaving me a shell of a person, totally void of feelings at such a young age. Pieces of my heart and soul scattered on the ground like shards of broken glass. Who talks to their kids like that? Bit by bit her words started to destroy what should have been a normal healthy parent child relationship of love, trust, comfort and guidance, but instead she replaced it with hate, fear, mistrust and abandonment. Where was God to protect me or shield me from her words that cut like a knife? Or maybe God doesn't visit Dorchester or the ghetto? However, the devil does! Trust me he does.

I wish I could say we had a normal home with a mother and a father, a nice house with a white picket fence, a typical life growing up, but we were far from that. We did not have a father, but we had an abusive mother and we lived in the projects. I do not remember any white picket fences growing up in the concrete jungle. Drug abuse, drinking, domestic abuse and sexual assaults surrounded us. The sick part of it all is that we thought it was normal and we believed everyone lived like us. Not your usual definition of normal, but for us it was all we knew. I thought everyone got their asses kicked a few times a day by their loving mother. I thought everyone tasted blood before school from the fists of their mother in anger. I just thought that was the norm, because we had nothing else to judge it by. The physical and mental abuse was an everyday thing. I never got a day or a holiday off, Christmas, Easter or my birthdays. They were all just another day full of chaos from life with my mother. Anything could set her off, she was a ticking time bomb. For example, if we didn't eat our dinner, she would come from behind us and smash our faces into our plates. Her motto was, you eat it or you wore it and she meant every word of it. Blood dripping into our dinner plate from our noses and we had to finish every bit of it, blood and all. My mother was tough; there were no breaks, no remorse and no forgiveness. If you were looking for forgiveness, you looked to the Lord, not my mother.

Every day after bath time, oh the dreaded bath time, she would pin us between her legs to brush out our hair with this wooden brush, this was a heavy ass brush. If we moved our heads at all, the brush would land upside our heads with such force it would make our ears ring and leave large welts. I had thick curly hair that was a bitch to untangle, she would just rake through it, pulling out hair and not stopping for tangles at all. I had so much hair ripped out of my head as a kid, it was unreal (I should be bald). Through the tears and sobs, I always tried to stay still, but my body would tremble with fear, because it could get worse, a lot worse, if I moved. It was nearly impossible not to move my head. Years later I would still flash back to that damn brush and the crack of it upside my head. It is funny how some things never leave you and haunt you for the rest of your life. Even a simple task of brushing your hair brings back terrifying memories of your youth. A hairbrush is your boogeyman, unbelievable. But the scars run deep, very deep.

In Dorchester, as a kid I remember being tied up with a harness on the back porch, like a dog. I had a small amount of space to play in, a few toys and that's all I was allowed for playtime. It didn't matter if it was snowing or bone-chilling cold from the bitter New England wind. Even in the blazing heat, weather so hot you could fry an egg on the sidewalk, that is where I was, on my little length of rope. I think the neighbor's dog had more room than I had and more toys. I think I was a little jealous of that dog to be honest. I think my mother did that to nurse her hangovers and make sure I didn't go anywhere, because who wants to deal with a young active kid when you have a hangover, right? Unlike my brother and sister (Whom my mother had scared shitless with the warning if they did anything wrong, they would be beat.) I was that kid that would go off on my own any chance I got, and a harness was a cheap babysitter. It was one of the many steps that took away my humanity, being tied up to a porch like a dog. When you are treated like an animal, you tend to become just that, an animal. I remember one day, my mother said I was such a fuck up, that no one wanted to watch me. She brought me to the local hospital and told me what to tell them. She had me act like my appendix was ready to burst. She told me to tell them I could not move and where to say the pain was, see, she was a nurse earlier in her life, but that was long ago. She knew what to say and what pains I should have. I heard her tell her friend she needed a break from me and had me admitted into the hospital. She just made Quincy City Hospital my babysitter. It was crazy. She was free for the weekend. But my mother knew how to manipulate people very well. She was the master of manipulation. The greatest puppet master there ever was. I spent my weekend at Quincy City Hospital getting prepped for surgery and my mother spent her weekend drunk at the Hillbilly Ranch, in downtown Boston (Thinking about it, what the hell was a Hillbilly Ranch doing in downtown Boston, seems a little out of place). My mother was a heavy drinker and drank often, and she would stay out until 3 am on the weekends. It was her home away from home. It's where she fit in. We both got a break from each other that weekend. It was a good weekend. Thinking back, it breaks my heart to think that I thought it was better getting ready for surgery and being cut into, then being around my own mother. I shake my head in disbelief looking back upon it now, how fucked up is it to have those feelings? I should have been thinking about riding a bike, catching frogs, not looking forward to being cut open just to have someone take care of me and the added bonus of getting away from my mother.

We lived off welfare and state handouts; USDA peanut butter, cheese and dried milk, like most of the poor families in the 70s. I just loved the peanut butter; you would always have to mix it up, because after you let it sit for a while the oil would come to the top like a big oil slick. Sometimes that's all we had in our cabinets and we would have to survive off that. Any spare money we had would go to my mother's weekends at The Hillbilly Ranch. My mother always said I would drive her to drink. You see I have ADHD and am a little hyper; I have always been full of energy. No focus, mind bouncing just like my body, always moving. I was a handful no doubt, but I was just a little kid, an innocent kid. We would have a babysitter on the weekends, and my mother would always return home late, drunk, and fighting with one of her boyfriends. We were happy to get a break from her and her abuse. I was always happy when she was gone, I could breathe and be a kid, only temporarily. It would all come to a halt when she walked through the door drunk. Reality kicked in with the slam of the back door, my mother stumbling in looking for a target for her rage and the abuse would start all over. It seemed like the alcohol would make her even meaner than she already was. If she did not have a boyfriend to fight with, she would wake me up and beat my ass, sadly, at this point in my life, I was used to it. I would pretend to be asleep shaking in my blankets, I would pray she had a boyfriend to fight with when she came home and she would leave me alone. Boy, did I pray. Some nights I was lucky and escaped her wrath, and other nights I got my ass beat. As I write this, I drift off in thought; images go streaming through my mind like a horror film that had no ending credits.

At 5 years old I feared my mother. All I wanted to do was get away from her. What 5-year-old wants to be away from his mother? None that I know of. My mother was beating me half to death and I was truly scared of this woman. I would flinch when she walked by, waiting for her to strike me. My mother was the monster waiting in the closet to jump out at me. A mother is supposed to keep the boogeyman away and keep you safe, not become your boogeyman. For some reason, I just made my mother so angry. I brought out the beast in her and I didn't know why. I guess I would just have that effect on her all the time. I ran away from home for the first time when I was 5 years old. I didn't get very far, under our porch to be exact, but when you are that little it's still a big distance. That's crazy when you think about it, even at that young age I wanted to get away. As I hid under the porch to our house, I was afraid she would kill me if she found me. What great thoughts to have when you are five years old, fearing for your life at the hands of your mother, absolutely crazy. I remember being cold, afraid and shivering. I was afraid of what my mother would do to me if she found me, and if she would finish what she started to do. I was so terrified at the thought. I could see through the cracks of the porch that the police and the fire department were looking for me. I was afraid she would really hurt me if I came out and returned home. I started to get so cold and scared that I came out of hiding and went straight to a police officer, thinking I could get some help. Instead, he brought me right back to my mother. My mother acted like there was nothing wrong and she really was really concerned, it was all an act. My mother was a great actress. That night was quiet, but the next day there was hell to be paid. I got my ass beat so badly I couldn't move for hours. I do not know if I could not move from the pain or just plain fear. Like a deer caught in the headlights of this monster. God was not under the porch with me that night when I needed him to protect me from this woman. I remember questioning why was this happening to me? Why did my mother hate me so much, what did I do to deserve this? I was 5 years old, what could I have done to her?

My mother was a large woman, and when I say large, I mean large. Over 350 pounds and she had the strength to back up anything she wanted to do. My mother always fought with her weight, she was a bigger woman and wanted to be skinny. She had a problem with being overweight, it definitely bothered her a lot and it showed. I think this brought her a lot of unhappiness and anger. Years later, she went for a stomach bypass- a bariatric surgery to lose weight, but it never really did much for her. I remember she would go to a few doctors around Boston and get diet pills. These diet pills would be sold to make ends meet, they were the speeders everyone took back in the day and highly sought after. It was just supplemental income to the welfare check.

She was always in and out of relationships and always spent time at the bars. It always seemed my mother would find weak men that she could manipulate or bend. She was a control freak. Dishes smashing, physical fights and loud screaming matches back and forth would always awaken us. I learned later, that my mother would take men home for money or something else; she would always gain something through these men. She would wake up with a hangover, and a new strange man by her side and it would be the worst time ever. She would be pissed off and I knew I was going to bear the brunt of it. She would walk by me and just punch me until I bled; it was her own little way of saying good morning to me. My childhood was lived in fear and abuse. I was scared all the time. What a way to mold a child. Teaching them to be scared, fearful of the one who was supposed to love and protect you. She was definitely not going to be voted mother of the year by any means, not even close, she missed it by a long shot.

In addition to her bar room hookups, my mother would also have these prison pen pals; she would receive money and letters through the mail from inmates in the state prison. I think she made good money and I think she liked the attention of the men. A very captive audience. They would tell her what she wanted to hear. I think it made her feel good about herself, even though the men were confined and were playing her for their own needs. It didn't matter to her, attention was attention. There was one guy named Bill and he was serving time for a murder in the 70s. I remember some weekends she would get a ride and take us kids to visit men in Walpole State Prison; strange men, scary men like Bill. She would bring packages to them and use us kids as decoys to get the packages by the guards. Who's going to watch for packages when three adorable children are in the room? Not that we minded being decoys, we didn't know we were decoys. We just knew we got to eat as much candy as we wanted. I could only imagine that with my ADHD/hyperactivity and then being all hopped up on candy, I was quite a show to watch and a bit of a distraction. It was another way my mother put us in harm's way for her benefit. She made money bringing these inmates drugs. I think she let men use her, because she wanted to feel wanted.

When we had free time, my brother Jimmy, sister Cindi and I, would go up the street and play around the back of the old stores of Dorchester. There was broken glass everywhere from the winos drinking & breaking their wine bottles against the buildings, there were used needles from the junkies shooting up, and just trash everywhere. Looking back, I can't even believe we thought that was a play area, but that is the city life for poor kids like us. I remember I was always falling off the roof of the store or out of a tree we used to climb onto the roof with and cutting myself on the glass below. We played with dirty needles, throwing them into the trees, like some sick game of darts and we did not know any better, we were kids. That was normal for us.

In the fall of 1971, my mother had another child, Denise with her boyfriend at the time named Lee. He was a good man and a bit of a drinker himself. Lee took a liking to me and tried to stand up to my mother about her abuse to me, but he soon learned to mind his own business, he was a victim of my mother also. They seemed to be fighting all of the time, if it wasn't one thing it was another with my mother. They were in an up and down relationship for a few months.

They played house and had a kid. I remember their last fight, drunk as usual and lots of yelling. When the police came, Lee was toted off in handcuffs. It was just another end to one of my mother's infamous fights and another bad relationship. I remember waking up the next morning looking for Lee's false teeth in the backyard where the cops threw him down on the ground and handcuffed him. It was par for the course you see, what happened with Lee, all of my mother's relationships ended badly. Another violent end to the rare calm that we temporarily enjoyed. I think she truly enjoyed the art of fighting, she was a champ. Life went back to same ole, same ole.

It seems like we were always behind on bills and could never make ends meet, just a part of growing up poor. There was never any money. We would get behind in rent and would be evicted. We bounced from home to home. See, being poor and a single mother, that is what you did and it was accepted as the norm. Everybody did it. We never had money for anything and we would always be behind on something or another. As I said earlier, we had a deadbeat dad that did not pay any support; we relied on government handouts and clothing stipends to get by. Life was hard growing up poor and it never seemed to get any easier. You never get a break from being poor, no vacations, and no toys like the other kids. If you have never been poor, you would never understand. It is the worst feeling for a kid watching other kids play with toys that were out of your reach. You never got clothes that were in style, because you always wore hand me downs or secondhand thrift store clothing. At Christmas, you always relied on some organization giving you handouts for toys. I guess the stores would donate them to the poor and get a huge tax write off. The cycle never seems to end, once you're poor that's the way it is... There was no escaping poverty, not for a second.

My mother always had another family living with us, another single mother with kids, I never understood why. Maybe someone to share the bills with, someone to hang out at the bar with, but we always had a family with us. She would say she was helping them, but I think they were in a bad place and she was too. Misery really enjoys company, especially when you are poor and living day to day, meal to meal, it was the way it was. Sometimes it worked out and other times it did not.

We never really saw my dad much, we heard stories about him and that was it. His family didn't have much to do with us either; we never knew our grandmother, aunts or uncles. We met them a few times growing up, maybe twice. I wouldn't have remembered them if we ever bumped into each other on the street. Only my grandfather on my dad's side had anything to do with us. The rest of my family on my father's side had cast him out after he divorced my grandmother. Nothing like having your family turn on you. I guess that was the price he paid for finding his own happiness. But he made a point of being a part of our lives and that meant the world to us kids. He would send us cards and put money in a bank account somewhere for us on our birthdays and Christmas. He was a good man and visited us every now and then. He would take us to McDonald's and buy us fries without any salt. He was an odd fellow, but a good man to say the least. If it weren't for him, we would never have eaten at McDonald's, that was only for kids with money... Not poor kids like us.

I remember moving to Mattapan, a part of Boston, right around the time I was seven. The abuse was the same, just a new place and new surroundings. But we managed to get to go out and play a little more. My brother and I always walked the river, the city was busy and that's where we would always find ourselves, at the river. My brother and sister were my best friends growing up, because we shared so much, the pain, the abuse and the fear, we always had each other. We were all we had, living in our nightmare that no one on the outside would ever understand. One day, I remember walking on the river, it was frozen over and my brother was walking behind me, because I was the younger brother and he wanted to keep an eye on me and make sure I was fine. I was always the first one to try something or go first into the unknown. I suddenly heard my brother scream and when I looked back, he had fallen through the ice and was submerged underwater. I could see his face through the ice as he was being pulled under it. I panicked, thinking I was going to lose him. I started pounding on the ice with anything I could grab and finally I was able to break through the ice and pull him back out. Remembering our walk home, we were soaking wet and were afraid for our mother to see us wet, cause we were going to get into trouble. I remember running through my head what we would say and being terrified, cold, shaking and in fear... I just almost lost my best friend and my brother, now I had to be scared of what my mother would say or do when she saw us wet. We sat outside freezing until we came up with a good enough excuse. Scared of what my mother would say about us being wet. Our mother was ruler and we were going to get our asses kicked regardless of what we said. We came up with an excuse and we still got beat. I was glad that my brother was safe and

I still had him, he was my best friend and I could count on him for anything.

While living in Mattapan we started school during the forced desegregation in Boston. In the 70's neighborhoods like Mattapan were being driven even further into poverty when the more affluent residents started moving into the suburbs. The schools weren't getting funding in the poor parts of town. So U.S. District Judge Arthur Garrity had signed an order requiring that kids be bused from the rich white neighborhoods into areas that were mostly black and poor like Roxbury or Mattapan. The black and poor kids would be sent to the rich area schools. This was supposed to balance things out. We were in one of the Mattapan school districts that had forced busing. From the frying pan into the fire. We had to take the bus out of Mattapan into a different area. I remember people fighting. People were throwing bricks at the buses and breaking the windows. It was crazy. The upper classes didn't want the blacks or the poor kids in their school districts, using their tax money. Little did they know, we didn't want to be there either. We were called names, threatened and spit at by so-called good, God fearing Christians? These were upper class mothers protesting, mothers who loved their children and never abused them. These same mothers threw stones at little kids, called them names and spit on all of them because they were from the wrong side of town. The situation quickly spiraled out of control that it quickly made the national news. Police were in riot gear on our elementary school buses. We had to have security with us all day long at the school. We walked through metal detectors and had to have police escorts to school. I did not ask for this, but some guy in a three-piece suit up on the hill decided this for me. The protest went on for months and the National Guard had to be called in just so little kids could go to school. God did not exist in the ghetto or on our bus route back then, that's for sure!

About a year later, we moved back to Dorchester, just a different part of town from where we lived before. My mother was having an affair with the man that owned the house we moved in to. I believed he was a married man; nothing was sacred to my mother. "Nothing". She was always in destructive and abusive relationships. Looking for love in too many faces. We moved back to a three family flat. I remember this time very well. Our first few nights were crazy. I remember waking one night to a rapist was being chased through our yard, he jumped through my bedroom window and was caught right there in our house. I woke up covered in glass and the police were everywhere. I remember finding a police officer's hat the next day and I thought that was the coolest thing.

My life remained the same, the physical abuse escalated and the verbal assault continued relentlessly. My mother's drinking continued to get worse and there was always a new guy coming and going, but it always ended the same way, fighting and more fighting. The abuse never seemed to take a break in my life, how I prayed for it to stop, but it never did. I am so surprised I made it this far as a kid. My mother would say that I would never make it to 10 years old, insisting that she would kill me. I was the only kid that had life insurance on them, did she know something or was she planning something. I laugh to myself now, how crazy this truly sounds, but this was normal to me. Maybe the reason she never connected me was due to putting her first child up for adoption. Anytime she felt forced into a corner, or a loss of control in a situation, it would send her into a spiral. Or maybe she didn't plan on me being around very long. There's nothing like growing up with the fear of your mother killing you. It's not very comforting. Now I think to myself, did she want me to believe that I was worthless and maybe kill myself, so that she could collect the insurance money and live a better life, I don't know. I know this may upset and bother many people in so many ways, but the truth is the truth. Anything that is done in the dark always finds its way to the light.

When I was seven, my father got married to my stepmother Cindy. Because her name was like my sister's name, we called her Big Cin. They started to come around a little, I think Cindy wanted it that way and she wanted us kids around. Cindy was a good woman and she tried to help with my father's drug abuse and the craziness that surrounded his life. I think if she hadn't married my father, we would never have seen him. Cindy always came to visit and hang out with us kids; she was the only woman that I ever saw stand up for us and especially to my mother. We were always happy to see her and my father. They would bring us gifts on our birthdays and at Christmas. My father and Cindy started to take us on the weekends and we always looked forward to spending time with them. When I was eight they had a son of their own, my brother Jason. Shortly after, things started to go sour like they always did when my dad was involved. This was too bad for us kids, as we didn't see him or Cindy as much anymore. It was not entirely unexpected with the type of behavior my dad exhibited our whole lives, but it was still a loss for us. Cindy really liked us and we liked her. When she was around, the abuse stopped. She was not afraid of my mother and we lost that when they split up.

When I was eight I started to get into more trouble, I remember throwing our mattresses out the window and jumping on them from the second floor window, the normal things that young boys did. In spite of everything, we were good kids and we had each other, but my mother never looked at us like that. We were an annoyance to her, a constant reminder of failures in her life, failed relationships and she couldn't be who she wanted to be. Who knows, it's like there was a hunger for more in her and we were just in the way. See, when you grow up poor, you always feel hungry, it just seems like you never get enough to eat, or there is always something missing in your life. The hunger isn't always about food. But it can cause the same feelings of emptiness in the pit of your stomach. With so many mouths to feed and so many kids looking to her for food – not just to fill our stomachs, but our hearts as well, it's easy to see why food was a control for my mother. At dinner, we had to clean everything off our plates or we wore it. I always ate my sister's food she did not eat, I hated the vegetables, but I hated my sister getting knocked around more. My sister Cindi would sit at her plate and I could see her hands tremble with fear that if she did not clean her plate off, she would have to face my mother's wrath. I never liked seeing her get beat or my mother being mean to her. She was my baby sister, I loved her and I felt like it was my job to keep her safe. When she did something wrong, I would say it was my fault and that I did it, it would break my heart to see Cindi cry or be hurt. It was the one thing that I did feel in a world of numb feelings. I love my baby sister and would do anything to protect her, anything. When she would get a beating from my mother and sent to her room, I would gather all of her stuffed animals and put on a puppet show. I could always make her laugh. It helped her forget what had happened moments ago, if only for a little while.

Even as I type this, my stomach wrenches, turns in knots and I get a cold chill running up my spine. To this day, I can still feel the pain I felt when she would get punished for an infraction of my mother's impossible to understand rules. It would tear my heart right out. I didn't see God sitting among us innocent kids then either, just like most times in my life he was noticeably absent. Where was God when my mother was beating my little sister Cindi? Not just spanked, but beaten and battered, for the smallest of infractions. I remember my mother calling her names all the time, calling her a little whore, as she was getting beat, but I never thought of the beatings I received. I get so angry typing this. It's so very shameful what my mother did to us as children. I can feel a tear trailing down my cheek as the memories of my childhood rise to the surface once again, rearing their ugly head of the abuse we suffered at our mother's hands. Please tell me where God was then.

While she was cooking, she would always take the hot ladle, sneak up behind me and put it to the back of my neck, burning me while I sat at the kitchen table doing my homework. I would always jump, I don't know if it was the surprise of the attack or the actual pain of the burning skin. Man, how do you do that to someone, never mind to a kid. My mother once threw a steak knife at me in our small kitchen, nearly missing my sister Cindi's best friend Kathy Barry. She apologized to Kathy but not to me. She constantly did little things like that all throughout the day. I received straight out punches to the back of my head, my mother was always sure to leave marks where you could not see them. Under my shirt or on my legs, but if her rage took over, I would get punched in the face and it would leave marks, but she was always ready to fill my head with an excuse, an explanation of why she did it. How I got the fat lip, bloody nose or black eyes. The lies always ran deep and she was ready to fill your head or someone else's with her lies.

I was 8 years old and I thought love was a punch in the gut or head. Every day was a beating; blood dripping from my nose, slamming my head into walls as she walked by, or she would kick me whenever she wanted to. I would be doing my homework at the table and she would come from behind and slam my head into the table. I would ask why with my nose dripping blood onto my book and she said, "You are just like your father," and then walk off. I was nothing like him. I was an innocent kid and didn't know my dad at all. I was paying the price for everything my father did to my mother. I wonder if God was watching and protecting me, if you asked me then I would have said no, no he wasn't. I was left to be unprotected and to be a protector to my brother and sister. I would cry myself to sleep every night shaking and afraid. Praying for someone to come and save us. But no one ever did, we were innocent kids and we were on our own. Nobody was there to protect us and no superhero was on the way to save us, this was our fate.

I remember one night Jimmy, Cindi, Denise and I were eating at the dinner table and I made a little mess. My mother flipped out. She filled the dog's dish with my dinner and had me eat off the floor of the kitchen, just like the dog would eat. I did it too, I guess fear makes you do some things you would never imagine doing. My mother used fear in every aspect of our lives. Fear is a terrible thing and can cripple and control you in numerous ways. It's healing in a way to have my entire childhood brought to light, the hidden secrets and abuse finally out in the open. It's truly liberating, this is the first time the entire story has been revealed. I am ashamed of her and feel a deep sense of embarrassment, didn't she know that she couldn't treat people that way. I worry about what people will think about my mother and our family all together, because of her actions. It leaves me feeling ashamed and guilty. I feel guilty because I am bringing to light a dark family secret, a secret that has been hidden for forty plus years.

My mother was very troubled and I wonder if she ever felt bad for what she did to us, the abuse and fear she instilled in us. On the outside, she would act like a good church going woman. She never stepped foot in church. But we kids were forced to go. We were forced to get our first communion, attend Sunday school and go to Mass every Sunday in Boston. We would have to bring home a flyer showing we were there. My brother Jimmy was an altar boy and I had to follow his example, I guess us kids showing up at church made her look like she was a good mother. We attended a church in Boston at a time when being an altar boy would lead to scandal. Years later we found out other altar boys were fondled in the church where we served as altar boys. One might ask where God was then. I never felt God's presence in that church and I'm sure those boys who were being molested, by supposed trusted members of the church, felt the lack of the Holy Spirit themselves.

CHAPTER 2

The Move to Germantown

W hen I was nine we received another eviction notice from Dorchester and my mother filed an application to get into public housing in Quincy, Mass. The one and only, the notorious G-town. Quincy was my birthplace and was right outside of Boston. Germantown would give me some of my fondest memories of growing up, some of my best friends, some people whom I consider family to this day. I also learned some of my hardest lessons on the streets of G-town, but I am a G town kid at heart.

Germantown was a small community, mostly made up of public housing and single mothers on welfare trying to get by. You could only get into Germantown one way; there was one way in and the same way out. It was a peninsula and surrounded by water on all sides. Germantown always smelled like Ivory soap, because the Procter & Gamble factory was across the water from Germantown and the scent would always drift over into our neighborhood. I hated the smell of Ivory soap for the longest time. The houses all looked the same, but were different colors in Germantown. Four families would share a single house that was broken down into four apartments. Very close living arrangements and you can only imagine the conflicts that ensued. There were always fights going on, if it wasn't parking spots, it was the noise, but everyone had something to bitch about. I guess it is expected, living that close together. There were also the few private homes on the outskirts of Germantown, for the families that could afford to own a house and didn't know anything about food stamps or food rations.

Most of the people in G-Town were good people going through hard times. See, being poor is a true struggle and it makes victims out of the less fortunate. We survived off food stamps to buy most of our food. Food stamps use to come in booklets and looked like money, for a long time, I thought food stamps were real money. What food we did not buy with food stamps, were state handouts. It's a big joke in G-town about cheese rations; there is no grilled cheese like the grilled cheese you make with government cheese, just the best. We had one local store in G-town called Lester's. A husband and wife, with a mean cat, owned it. They would let us spend our food stamps there on candy. My friends and I would steal food stamps from our mothers, walk down to Lester's and buy candy. The candy counter was huge. The counter had to be ten foot long. It was a glass case filled with a million different candies. We had pocketfuls at a time, I felt rich when I had a pocketful of candy. Picking out our candy was a break from the struggles of everyday life and we spent hours doing it as Mr. Lester waited on us. My friends and I would mix and match our candy together. It was a cool walk to Lester's and we always had time to talk, walk the seawall that protected us from the water that surrounded us and jump the pillars along the way, and trade our candy. One of my better memories, from that time in my life, was just being a kid without a care in the world.

We also started to go to a new church when we moved to G town, called St Boniface. The church served the locals in Germantown. Just like before, my mother never attended, we had to attend and we had to bring home flyers to prove we'd been there. God forbid if we forgot to bring home our fliers, there would be hell to pay. Sometimes we would sneak in, grab a flyer and skate off to do other things with our friends.

As we started our lives in Quincy, my mother still drank often and the abuse never seemed to stop, it just got worse with time. It seemed like she always had a new boyfriend at the house, fighting and carrying on. The verbal and physical abuse only continued to escalate, but the beatings didn't have the same effect as they used to. I don't know if you get numb to the pain and it just doesn't affect you like it once did. I got to the point where I expected it and almost looked forward to it in a sick way. I guess it was some form of attention and I received very little if any, positive attention. So the negative had to suffice, it was attention, right? Once my mother realized she was losing that control over me, she would try harder to hurt me with her words. I think my mother's words always cut deeper than the scars she left on my body, my body would heal, but the memories of the words she would hurl at me like barbs of wire still haunt me to this day. Echoing in my head and making me second-guess everything. I always second-guess my self-worth and choices. Even today as a grown man. As

I sit here writing this, I think back to that little kid, so abused and scared. When she would call my name, I was so scared, I would pee my pants in fear. The scars I had to nurse, the memories I carried on in life, and my brother and sisters pain it all washes over me in great sorrow. I wish I could go back and tell that kid, "Everything is going to be alright, stay strong and it will get better". I see him just as clear today, as if it was yesterday. When I was banged up from her abuse, she would tell people I was clumsy or accident-prone. Despite her lies, a few close people and the neighbors knew the truth. I think they secretly felt bad for me, but would never say a word; my mother was a very controlling and vindictive person. If you crossed my mother, there was a price to be paid and it was never pretty. She was the nicest person to your face, but behind your back, she was mean and would go out of her way to hurt you. You would be blindsided and never suspect it was her, yes, she was very mean. Her mean streak ran deep like an endless well of pure hate and maliciousness. People tried to keep her on their good side.

There is a lot of abuse in the lower income neighborhoods, I guess it is accepted and not talked about much. It is accepted as a way of life and never confronted; you mind your own business and you stayed out of other people's business. Poverty breeds child abuse, domestic violence, sexual assaults, drug abuse and helplessness, it's a part of the culture. Very few make it out to live better lives. I had learned that getting out of the house was the best way to keep out of my mother's grasp and her ugly words she would spew at me. Anytime I was leaving out the door, she would attack me with her words or hit me again like I would somehow forget how worthless she thought I was. I look at my kids today and wonder how she did what she did to me, because I love my kids so very much and would die for them, unconditional love, 100 percent. Their lives mean more to me than my own. The only time I had to myself was at school during recess; I could act like a kid and keep my shield down.

I went through life on high alert always, shaking and afraid. Just waiting for the bomb to drop, you knew it was coming, you never knew when.

I started fifth grade at a new school called Snug Harbor, the school was located right in Germantown and was an easy walk from our house. We always had a time limit to get to school and we had to be back home within a certain time, if we were late, we got an ass kicking. God forbid if we had a little time to have fun with our friends, but again, that was all about control with my mother. She continually had to have control over us kids and she controlled us with fear. It's crazy what fear can do to a young kid, emotionally and physically. I was always late, always, and I paid for it. I always made friends quickly, I guess I had to be a people pleaser, or fly under the radar to keep the abuse I suffered a secret; plus we always seemed to be moving. We would be moving away soon enough I thought. As I started Snug Harbor, I had a few good friends that were close, Stephen, Ronnie, Phil and my brother. My friend Stephen was another abused kid like me. His father would beat him and treat him like a dog; I guess that's why we hit it off so well. We had a lot in common. Abusive parents that wanted nothing to do with us. His abuse seemed so bad to me, but I guess that's because I was so used to mine, that it seemed normal for me. I always said, if I ever had kids, they would never receive so much as a spanking from my hand in anger.

I started to get into a little trouble around Quincy. Stephen (Rosey, we called him Rosey, because Stephens last name was Rose.) was always by my side, he was my best friend and my partner in crime. I would skip school and go to the dog pound and watch all the dogs in their kennels and jump creeks all day. It was better than sitting in class all day. I always loved animals and being around animals. One day I asked the guy who worked at the dog pound where did all the dogs go. He explained that if they did not find a home, they would put them to sleep. Wow, did that hit hard. I thought about it and I just could not shake it, I guess I could relate to them, we were both abused and no one wanted us. The next night I broke into the dog pound, released every dog they had and threw their tranquilizer guns in the creek. I guess that was my way of making things right or even striking back for the abuse we both suffered. I think that night when I released the dogs, I also released something inside me, and maybe a little pain or suffering, I felt good. I was an animal lover and did not want to see any dog lose its life because it could not find a home. The police came to my house the next day because the officer knew it was me and told my mother to keep me away from the dog pound. He didn't want me to get into trouble for doing the right thing in a roundabout way. Just thinking about the dog officer chasing 50 dogs around Quincy makes me laugh. I got my ass beat for embarrassing my mother and having the police come to the door, but I don't think I felt anything through my grin while getting my punishment dished out to me. I felt like I struck back and felt vindicated. The good guys won! I got back into the swing of life, but never forgot that night of the big escape!

Germantown was a great place and I was proud of being a resident there, 214 in my heart forever. 214 was the bus number we would take into G town and buses were our way of getting out of and into G town. Most of the families didn't own cars, including us, cars were a luxury, and we were too poor to own a car. You couldn't buy a car with food stamps. It wasn't G town that was great, it was the people who took pride in where we lived, and we made G town what it was. Other towns looked down on us, but we were all proud to be from G town. If you live in a shit hole, but if you have pride in said shit hole, it becomes something bigger and better. We loved one another, we treated everyone like family and everyone knew everyone. It was a great place to live as a kid. We were the 214 G town and proud of it. At home was a war, but once we got out of the house, the kids in our neighborhood were our family and we always looked out for each other. Things were getting really bad at home; my mother was getting more abusive with her words. I took the brunt of her rage; so I decided it was time for me to leave and try to do things differently, time to do it on my own. What was I thinking; I was an 11-year-old kid, planning on running away. I fought with myself for a long time about running away. I knew I had to get away from my mother and find somewhere safe. I knew if I ran away, the abuse I received on a daily basis would be aimed at my baby sister or my brother. How could I feel good leaving and knowing how pissed off my mother would be, and leave her with two targets of opportunity. I know with me being gone, my brother and sisters would take the beatings that were intended for me. It made me sick to my stomach. Do I leave to protect myself, or do I stay and protect my siblings? I decided to run; I was left with no choice. I was forced to grow up at a very young age.

I ran away from home at the age of 11, I lived in burnt out buildings in downtown Boston that were abandoned and always smelled like smoke and urine. Stephen ran away with me and we met other kids that were in the same predicament as us, we banded together like a family of some sort. We all looked out for one another and ran the streets all night. The smell of smoke would cling to our hair and clothes from the burnt out buildings we slept in. I can still smell the scent of it today in my mind. I guess the smell will never leave me. I would walk the subway tunnels all night with friends. Some nights I was so cold, I could not keep my teeth from chattering or my body from shaking. The burnt out buildings would be infested with rats and you would have to try to get off the ground so the rats would not bite you. I think about it today and it breaks my heart and sends chills down my spine, I would never want any kid to go through that, to be so alone and have no one to turn to at such a young age. It's like waking up in the middle of the night to a bad dream, just to find no one is there to comfort you or tuck you back into bed. No kid should feel abandoned at that age. At the age of 11, there isn't much for you to do or too many options for you, no jobs or places to live. I would eat at the soup kitchens sometimes with the homeless people of Boston. It was always a sandwich and a cup of soup to carry you over. I ask how in society we get so lost that we let kids like me slip through the cracks and nobody notices. I met so many kids on the streets of Boston that fell through the cracks of the system. Our children are our future, not some disposable commodity. My mother finally had to report me as a missing child to the court system and then the cops were always looking for me. She would not report me missing, because the state would cut down on her food stamps and government rations. So most of the time I went unreported to the authorities for months at a time. It seems like this went on forever. I remember these days like they were yesterday, but they were a lifetime ago.

So, I had to survive and avoid the police, the same police that were supposed to help kids like me, a kid in need, were now hunting for me as a delinquent. It's kind of ironic when you think of it. I would periodically take the train back to Quincy. When I got to my house, my sister Cindi would sneak food and clothes out of the house for me when she could without getting caught. When you grow up like I did, you watch your food pretty good and boy did my mother. If my sister had ever gotten caught, my mother would have beaten her to no end for helping me. I remember one day a cop arrested me for C.I.N.S., I was locked in a cell, and I was afraid, cold and alone again. I kind of felt like those dogs I released at the dog pound. I was locked in a concrete room with a big wooden door with a ten-inch window. Every now and then a cop would look through the window and that was the only human contact I had. The next day I saw a judge and was considered a C.I.N.S., a child in need of services. I was brought to a foster home for kids like me, but these kids were not like me, they were bullies and they ran in cliques. The next day I decided it was not for me and I chose to leave. I hatched a plan to leave that night. As everyone went to sleep, I put my plan into motion, I crept out the back door and I was finally free of this foster home. I just did not fit in anywhere. Not home, not foster care, not anywhere that a normal 11 year old should fit in. I was back on the streets again, with the authorities keeping a closer eye out for me after escaping the group home or foster care. Back to the burnt out buildings with the rats running by at night and back to begging for food on the streets during the day. I didn't see God there in the faces of the other people fighting to survive on the streets with me.

After living on the streets for a few months, I was finally caught again and brought before a judge. He decided to send me to a long-term group home. I was there with 20 other kids just like me. Kids that were abused and throwaways. There were five counselors for the lot of us. Anchor House was for troubled kids, kids that would run away from their homes and get into trouble. Thinking about it, my mother needed a group home herself. I had a counselor named Ed. Ed was a good guy, but he had a dope habit. I know a kids group home and I end up with the one counselor who has a dope habit, who would ever have imagined. As I write this, I keep thinking to myself, you just cannot make this shit up, really. I guess it is hard hiring good help on a state budget. He would take me on day trips to the trap house, (the trap house is where all the addicts go to shoot dope and buy dope and hang out with prostitutes). He would tell the main guy at the program he was helping me with homework or some other excuse, like every dope addict out there. At the ripe old age of 11, I knew what a dope habit was, what skin popping was and what a shooting range was. How prostitutes worked and what they worked for. The prostitutes would always watch over me while Ed would nod off or shoot up. Where was God then? He was never in the dope houses we visited. I was very confused on what a "good" life was supposed to be. The man, who was supposed to be helping me become a good kid, was taking me places no kid should ever be in. My counselor would always take me with him, and he would always give me something special for keeping my mouth closed. I never told anyone where we went or what he was doing and he would always take me. I guess we had a little weird trust thing going on. Ed filled a role in my life I never had, a male figure trying to help me, dope sick and all. A dope sick counselor was my first male role model, man was I confused. I kind of felt like part of a family at the group home. Granted my father figure was an addict and the mother figures that watched over me peddled their bodies for another fix. It was safe and no one was hitting me or calling me names. I know that sounds off the wall, but that is how fucked up I was when I was a kid. At the Anchor house we did things, like go to the museum, and the YMCA, you know, things your parents should have done with you.

I was returned back to my mother's care after I graduated the group home and I completed my programs. At the age of 11, I had been through two group homes, arrested a few times, been in more dope houses and experienced more abuse than most people would ever understand. It seems like the only thing I knew about life was, there was no escape from the pain and suffering. No one wants to face the abuse of kids. It carries an ugly face and is always brushed under the carpet of life. Back in the day, it was accepted as the norm, a way to keep your kids in check. I had spent way too many days in the hospital, getting patched up and broken bones mended to be in any kind of check. Like I said, my mother had a golden tongue, knew what to say, and had an excuse for everything. He fell out of a tree, fell off his bike or something that fit the injury, unbelievable, didn't anyone see the truth behind the lies. Nobody is that lucky to beat a kid this many years and not get caught, but she was. I was always getting stitches or a cast put on. Come on, no one could see past her deception, no one? She should have been arrested and put away.

I was 12 years old when my mother filed paperwork with the court to have me declared an out of control youth. She didn't file it because she thought they would help me, but so she wouldn't get into trouble. It was simply to cover her own ass. How do you explain that your 12-year-old son lives on his own in the burnt out buildings in Boston? Why was I out on the streets freezing and begging for food. Especially when the state was giving her food stamps to feed me? So she filed the required paperwork and I was committed to the Department of Youth Services. I was assigned to DYS lockdown for troubled kids and they were going to show me who was boss or so they thought. They just did not understand that for the last 12 years I lived in hell, pure hell, give it your best shot. I lived with the monsters that would haunt normal kids at night. The pain that would take your breath away was normal for me, you see, I was truly damaged goods. At 12, I was one of the youngest kids to be committed. I was given a social worker named Howard and he was a good man, very old and wise. He seemed to be on my team, but time would tell. He was on the verge of retiring and just seemed like he wanted to surf through without any effort. He was sick of doing what he was doing and when you were caught, then he would just "deal" with you. When I was finally found and arrested, I was brought to Brockton YMCA. DYS had a locked down floor, on the 5th floor of the Y for youth offenders. Brockton YMCA had a group home feel much like Anchor House. The other kids that were there were getting into trouble and runaways, so I fit right in.

But now they put me with criminals who bragged about what they did and how they did it. While I was there, I learned more about being a criminal and how to get away with it. I was learning the ropes from the pros, the older kids. I heard stories from the other kids about how they made money on the streets and where they would live. Now this was the kind of school I could get behind. I learned how to be smarter and what to do to not get caught. The tricks of the trade so to speak. It was the beginning of my criminal education on how to run the streets. DYS and my mother sent me to learn to be a criminal and learn from the best.

Eventually, I got sick of the YMCA. So after 90 days of sitting around, I decided it was time to leave. I came up with a plan to escape. We were going to gym time, which meant they had to take you down a flight of stairs that led into areas with the public. On the way down, I took off and ran through an alarmed door and onto the streets of Brockton. I got away and I made it back to Quincy, back to G town, back to my comfort zone. While I was a runaway, I learned a few habits from the other kids. I learned how to steal clothes and other things, things to survive. I was too young to get a job and it was easier to take what I wanted. I guess when I was caught, they would just send me back to DYS and my caseworker. I know this sounds off the wall, but DYS kind of became my family. They seemed happy to see me when I got arrested, they didn't abuse me or call me bad names. I always had a bed and I knew I was safe, I was locked in and my mother and the world were locked out.

I was always running away from one thing or another my whole young life, but I was always left with my thoughts and myself. I could run away from a lot but I could never run away from myself and that voice in my head telling me I was totally worthless and I would never amount to anything, the physical and the deeper emotional ones. I was finally caught and arrested for stealing cars. I learned while in DYS Brockton, I could steal cars and sell them to the chop shop for good cash, so that's what I did. I went to court and was given probation. My probation officer was Don, he could see right through my mother and her abuse, he really tried to help me, she would always tear him down and call him names, not to his face, but behind his back. She would call him a homosexual, a fag and so on. She even abused my probation officer, as I said before no one was safe from my mother's wrath. I just think she didn't like him because he was trying to help me and keep me on the straight and narrow. If you saw anything good in me, my mother hated you and would try to destroy you, like she had done to me my whole life. God forbid I got any help in my life. The calm lasted a few weeks at my mother's house again. My mother's drinking had gotten worse. She would return home so drunk she would fall out of the taxi and us kids would have to help get her in the house. She would come in with a new guy and I would be up all night listening to them having sex or fight. There was always a new guy, like she needed to be wanted, by anyone, as long as she was wanted. I ran away from home again, away from her, and went back to living in the streets of Boston. Back to running with the tough kids, which was all I knew, that was the family that would not turn on me. Like before, I would travel back to Quincy to have food and my clothes snuck out by my sister Cindi. She was always looking out for me, one way or another. My sister Cindi has always had my back. She was my angel and to this day, she still is. I couldn't say thank you enough for being a tiny glimmer of hope in the darkness back then.

When I was found this time, I was arrested and held until I could see the judge. I was remanded to Roslindale. You pull up to this brick building, which looks like any school in any town. The outside hid a horror show inside. Roslindale Youth Center was the biggest hellhole and they locked children up in there. A DYS lockdown for the worst kids, I was 12 in a murder lockdown. These kids were tough, I mean tough. One kid was there for murdering his parents. You sat around all day doing nothing. What a tough lockdown. It was a shithole holding pen for the worst youth offenders. Once you were left there, it was like they forgot about you. It felt like you were on the island of misfit toys from that one Christmas special. When they had nowhere else to send you, they sent you to Roslindale. You sat in your "room" all day, which was really just a cell. Roslindale was so bad. The way they treated the kids in there, was nothing but pure evil. The place had a history of abuse and treating the kids, some as young as seven, as throwaways. This place was a living hellhole right here on earth and I wonder why they never were investigated or shut down. Where was God to watch over these kids who already have been given up on, abused and treated less than human?

I sat there for 2 months and I was offered a program called Outward Bound. Outward Bound was a 60-day program for troubled youth, where they would teach you survival skills and to trust in each other.

Everything was based on trusting your group and yourself. For a kid who grew up learning not to trust anyone, oh boy, this was going to be a challenge. Every morning you did a one-mile run, they would chip a hole in the ice and drop you in! What a way to start a day, but hey, you were awake. I learned how to rappel and count on others to survive. It was an awesome program and I felt a great sense of accomplishment completing this program. I finally completed something good in my life. I was returned to my mother's house once again and all the positive things that had come from Outward Bound faded away, just like everything good in my life. Anything that I did positive in my life; the abuse would always overshadow it and leave me back in the dark. I started hanging with my friend Stephen and we would go do things normal kids would do, walk the beach, build forts, and go to school. I was introduced to smoking weed and I loved it. It would take me away from my reality. The pain I held in my heart faded away, it would render me as numb to reality on the outside as I felt on the inside.

It always started good at my mother's house. It would seem like she changed. But that was never the case. The peace never stayed that long, the storm was always creeping back in, slowly, but surely. It was as if when she beat me, it was her way of showing me love. I guess attention, whether negative or positive, is still attention and I strived for attention. I know that sounds fucked up to a normal thinking person, but it was true, I really thought love was abusing someone, a punch in the face or a bad word that tore you down. Stephen went through a lot of the same things as me, the abuse, the beatings, the name calling, we were a lot alike and we often ran away from home together. Stephen and I had each other's back throughout our childhood. It seems like we spent most of our teen years running from one thing or another. We were not wanted at home, but the police for trying to avoid home wanted us, it was a confusing time to say the least. The nice thing about Boston was the transit authority (The T). You could get on a bus in G town and make it to the other end of the state in a few hours. It seemed like we were always on the move or getting into some kind of trouble. You could always stay warm riding the train all day. Plus, it was like a new adventure every day.

You see, my mother always looked normal on the outside. She would volunteer for this and that, she was a model mother in front of people, the school, the courthouse and her friends. However, abusers have many faces and blend in so well. I sit here and I think, was she a bad woman or was she a good woman with a lot of problems? Did I do something to bring all that hate to the surface, or was she damaged a long time ago? What were her demons? Or was I just a bad kid? Where was God to save me? Where was God to show my mother how to be a good mom or save her from her demons? The physical scars would always heal, it didn't matter how deep they were, the scars always healed. But the mental scars would never heal. You might get past them, but they are always there haunting you and reminding you what you went through.

As I sit here writing this, I still feel fear, fear she will see what I am writing. Fear that I'll bring some kind of hidden truth to the surface of what other secrets might be buried with her. She has been dead for several years and the fear is still a tangible thing. What happens if she finds out the abuse still affects me to this day and in every way? It's crazy how bad you can screw a kid up at such a young age. Even into my late 40s, the specter of my mother's rage still had a negative effect on me

I am ashamed, I always wanted people to think I had a good life and came from a normal family, but that is so far from the truth. Don't get me wrong, there were good times every now and then, but so few memories of the good. The bad just washed them away. I watched the good times flowing out to the sea like the tide. This shit has affected me for my entire life.

Joseph C Hirl

CHAPTER 3

A Childhood Lost

The next few years ran the same course, I was returned to my mother, and I ran away, got committed to DYS, returned to my mother and then ran away again when stuff started getting bad. She always had a hold on us kids, through fear, and fear alone. No one wanted to go up against her. I remember when she would take us to the beach, she would bring my brother and I out to the deep part of the water. There she would hold us underwater until we would gasp for air; I really believe she wanted to kill us. Who holds their children under water until they gasp for air, the air that gives them life? Thinking back on this, I call my brother Jimmy and ask him if he remembers this and what effect it had on him. Jimmy still remembers this until this day. His voice cracks as he said he did not know why she did that to us, but he remembers it like it was yesterday. He remembers watching her drag me out into the water at the beach, until I was over my head and could not touch the bottom. He said the water had to be at least 2 feet over my head, and then she would leave me there. Jimmy said he was always afraid that he was going to watch me drown and our mother would make it look like an accident. I truly think she wanted me to die to get the insurance money. It should be second nature to protect your child and keep him out of harm's way. I remember that was one of the most terrifying moments of my life. I was screaming at the top of my lungs while water rushed into my mouth. I kept sinking to the bottom of the water and shooting back up. I could feel my lungs fill with water and the sting of my nose as I breathed in the salt water. I was truly ready to die, just give up and let my body float away. It's a good thing the tide was coming in, because that is what saved my life, not my birth mother but Mother Nature. Wow, I sit in this chair after I get off the phone with Jimmy and think back to those days so long ago. Days at the beach, which should be happy memories for kids, are just another nightmare for me. I can remember the taste of the salt water, the sting in my nose, how the sun reflected off the waves, I hear the waves coming in and I get lost in thought. It leaves me angry and a little bit shaken. These sick people run around our world every day. They blend in, pure evil waiting to strike. Things went on like this for years and it surprises me that I am still alive. I laugh to myself in a sick kind of way, thinking I beat her at this, I survived!

As life went on, I had a few girlfriends, puppy love since I never knew how to accept true love. I would always push them away. I never let anyone get close to me. I didn't love myself or even like myself. I guess I was brainwashed into thinking I was a horrible person. Thinking I would never amount to anything and no one would ever love me. My mother really had messed me up in the head.

Like I said, the scars run deep and I was so very fucked up. I just wanted to appear like a normal person on the outside, but on the inside I was the biggest mess. People just could not see it, the mess I was, I hid it well. See, when you're being abused whether you're a kid or anyone really, you start to believe the lies of the person who is abusing you. You learn to cover up the bruises or tell stories about what happened to you, I fell off my bike, or I was roughhousing with my brother. You cover for them, because in your head you think you deserve it, after all, you're a no good fuck up right? The worst part is knowing that if people start looking too close, they might ask questions. Questions could lead to an investigation, and oh boy, if someone shows up at the door, you better believe the next beating will be like nothing you've felt before. So you learn early on to hide it, don't say anything and don't let people get to close. Like they always say, the house might look good from the outside, but it's really a mess on the inside. I would always be returned to my mother though. She was the great actor in front of people, the caring mother, and she always said the right things and played the part of a caring mother so well. It's funny, but later on in life, my sister's friend told me that she didn't know Cindi and Jimmy had a brother Joey. I was always locked away in DYS or on the run. It was as if I never existed, they never saw me growing up, no pictures on the wall and I was never around the house. That really hurt. Then I realized I was gone more than half my life, running from the abuse, authorities or something. Had I turned into that beast my mother always said I was or was I just a fucked up kid?

I was never in school much, especially throughout middle school. I was absent all the time in 6th and 7th grade because I was being sent to DYS, running away or something or another. I dropped out of school in the beginning of 8th grade. My brother Jimmy was always into sports and he did well, I think my mother found some pride in him. She could point to Jimmy and say he was on this team or another and it made her look like a normal mother. I was more into nature, chasing frogs, hanging out and building forts. Every chance I got to go outside, I would stay out for hours. My mother looked at me differently because of this, I guess. I don't know if she just couldn't understand that my brother and I were different people, or if I just wanted to be outside where I felt safe.

I was 13 and living out of basements in G town. The basements were dirty and always smelled like piss and cats. I had a lot of good friends that would help me and I could always count on my sister Cindi to sneak me out food so I could eat. How I prayed to have a normal life, like some of my friends I had gone to school with. I looked at their lives like I used to look at all that candy at Lester's. But that was never going to happen, not as long as they kept sending me back to my mother. This was my normal, on the streets hustling for a living.

I stuck around Germantown. I knew everyone and everyone looked out for each other. I was a tough kid; in my neighborhood I was always fighting someone. I started to have no feelings for anyone, like I had a wall built around me and no one could ever penetrate it. I was numb to the world around me. The wall kept everyone out, and it was my defense. Can't touch me. Things that used to bother me or hurt me were buried deep inside. I had to become heartless and indifferent, it was my key to survival. I had to look out for myself first. Imagine being 13 and having to harden yourself to everything just to live another day? I think back about this time of my life and realize it was truly when the monster, my mother always said I was, started to rear its ugly head.

There was so much to do down in G town, we always stayed busy and the people were great. On the weekends when I was home from lockdown, we would get out of the house and try to be kids. There was the pier to swim off and hang with the neighborhood kids. We would swim over to Proctor and Gamble, jump off their loading docks, where they would fill the ships with that damn Ivory soap. Or we would go up to the Quincy quarries and jump off the cliffs. A lot of friends died there. But it didn't stop us.

I met some new friends, but Stephen was always my best friend and someone I could count on. He had my back through thick and thin. We were fourteen now and we were kids of the night. We would creep around in the shadows, stealing things, like cars. We could make money stealing them and it seemed easy enough. We would catch the T into Boston and the Dorchester crew taught us the best way to tilt cars and steal them. We ran with the older kids, being lookouts for them and doing the stuff they didn't want to do. We ran with both the South Boston kids and the Dorchester kids, always finding something to do. Living in cars and old abandoned apartments.

As I turned fifteen, I was returned home once again, but nothing had changed. I did my best to please my mother, but there was no pleasing that woman. She had no happiness in her own life, how could she be happy for anyone else. She was more abusive every time I came back, it's as if she hated me more for having a break from her anger and it was still there, waiting for me. Her words would always cut deep and would cut often; nothing was off limits to her. If I was talking with a girl, she was a whore and unworthy to talk to. She would try to take every bit of happiness away from me. I guess for the longest time I didn't know what love was or how to love someone or to have someone love me. I was really devoid of feelings or thoughts of happiness. I lived in darkness my whole young life and I never felt the warmth of the sun on my face. I was pretty screwed up to say the least. The abuse would get so bad that I had no choice but to leave again. I was afraid one day she would kill me. I would live out of basements of G town, a friend's house and just walk the streets all night. The streets were my comfort zones. I knew how to keep myself safe and I always had my friend Stephen to hang out with. We would keep each other company and look out for each other. The people of G town would always have your back and we had a friend Mary who had her own apartment there. Mary would always make sure we were fed and had a warm place to sleep, but my mother ruined that too. She would find out Mary was helping us and report her to housing. Any safe zone we found, my mother was quick to take it away from us, proving to us that there was no escaping her control. I never received a second of peace.

I got caught stealing cars a few times and I was locked away. I was always returned to my mother I always held out hope that maybe something was going to be different this time, maybe she had a change of heart and realized the error of her ways and she would love me. But that wasn't the case. I remember making it through the week and on Saturday mornings she would have us all clean. It was our Saturday morning routine. She would put on her 8 track and we would clean to Engelbert Humperdinck. We all had our chores to do, Jimmy had the bathroom to clean, Cindi had the living room and her bedroom to clean, Denise had her room to clean and I had my room to clean. I remember one time I threw all my stuff under my bed and I guess she knew it. She told me she was going to kill me if there were any clothes under my bed. She called my sister Cindi to go up to my room and told her to look under my bed. If there was anything under it and she didn't tell her, she would get the same as me. I never saw such fear in my sister's eyes, I knew she wanted to protect me, but she was too afraid to lie and get the punishment I had coming. She had to tell the truth, I was just thinking what am I going to get beat with, the race car track, the belt or fist, or all the above. I think my mother just looked for something to beat my ass over, not like she needed a reason to do so.

By sixteen I was starting to get my adult height, and the physical abuse started to slow down. I was over six feet tall and not a skinny little kid anymore. My mother had to resort to the words that were at times more cutting than any physical blow she ever dealt me. She would throw her abusive words at me, but they wouldn't stick, not anymore. So she would go after other people in my life, like a girlfriend or someone trying to help me in my life. If I had a good friend, she would call him a queer and ask if we were boyfriends, or if I had a girlfriend, she would call them a whore or they were this and that. Anything that I cared about, she wanted to tear down and take away from me. Anything I felt comfort in, she did not like and she destroyed it. She never had a kind word for anyone, I learned about this time, her life was pretty bad also growing up. You think she would want better for her own children, not the same fate that she endured. My mother was forced to raise her brother and sisters in her youth, her parents had treated her like shit and put her down her whole life. I guess I could understand a little where she came from and what made her so angry, maybe she was just sick of raising kids. I don't know. I guess I felt bad for her, but I knew she would never change. She was always going to be the same person she was, until "she" decided to change and I did not see that coming anytime soon.

I started to get into even more trouble as I grew up. I was 17 and got picked up for stealing cars and a few B&E's. I was sentenced to the big league now. I was sentenced to Dedham House of Correction for adult offenders. I was sentenced to 90 days. When I pulled up it looked like an evil castle. I was scared and didn't know what it held for me. As I did my 90 days, I met more skilled criminals. All they talked about is what they got away with and how they did it. It was like a school for the older criminals to teach younger criminals the right way to be a criminal, but also to teach them new tricks. With the new people I met in Dedham, came a completely new networking system. New contacts, new tricks up my sleeve and a complete education. I was released and I started right back down the same road, stealing cars, hanging out and drowning my feelings with drugs, booze and anything else that would dull the pain I had in my heart.

I met a girl named Denel, she was from the good part of G town and she was a good girl with a good family. The first time I saw her, I thought to myself, she looks like an angel and I started to talk with her, but she didn't want anything to do with me. She told me right from the start, I know you Joey Hirl and I am not falling for you. She was right, I was trouble and I had a lot of people who didn't want anything to do with me. I was a problem child from the wrong side of the tracks. I guess she saw something in me, something worth saving or maybe she just had a Mother Teresa moment, but we started dating.

She really fell for me fast, but she didn't know how truly screwed up and damaged I was. She didn't know that I didn't know how to love a person or even care about a person. Or that the scars from my mother would never let me love a person like her. I didn't think I was worthy of anyone loving me. If you loved me, there was a different agenda or angle. She would try to protect me from the world. She would lend me her car so I wouldn't go boosting a car. She would hide me out when I was wanted by the police. She went above and beyond to help me, but I never understood it. Everyone else saw how self-destructive I was and tried to get us to go our own ways. Her dad had a strong dislike towards me, he saw the path I was on and wanted to keep me away from his daughter. He wanted to find me and make the point himself. I was a tough guy and I did not care. He was a black belt and he had wise guy connections, neither one fazed me for one second. I am sure he would have made his point clear.

As I turned 19, we hung with a group in G town and started to party pretty heavy ourselves. I was introduced to cocaine and I started to do it all the time. It seems like if there was an escape to be found, I was there. I dragged Denel with me, straight in a downward spiral. She was trying to save me and I was trying to destroy us, what a combo. The harder she tried to pull me back from the edge, the more determined I was to take us both over it. She never gave up on me. No matter how much grief I caused her, she kept trying to save me from myself.

I kept getting into trouble stealing cars and I was wanted again. A few friends and I thought it would be a good idea to go to Atlantic City and hide out. We took a bus there and Denel made sure I had money, as I said she was my great protector. We hung out on the boardwalk and would eat at the casinos, plus they gave away free drinks. After a few weeks, I missed home and wanted to come back to G town. We were out of money and just wanted to be on our own home turf. That night we decided to steal a car and come home. We started walking the boardwalk and we found a Monte Carlo SS. The only way to get the car on the main drag was to ride up on the boardwalk like the police did. I stole the car and brought it up on the boardwalk until I came to an opening to the main drag. To this day I don't understand what I was thinking or why I didn't get caught, I mean really, the Atlantic City boardwalk? On the way home, we would fill the car up full of gas and take off. I think we had $20.00 to our name.

We made it back to Boston. As we drove into Southie, we decided to stop and get something to eat. I ran in and grabbed the food. On the way out, I saw the Boston police department had the car surrounded with guns drawn. I dropped the food and ran. I got away and I had Denel pick me up. I learned later on, that a car like the one we stole was involved in a bank robbery earlier that day. There had been a shootout, between the cops and the robbers. Turns out the car we boosted in Atlantic City fit the description of the getaway car to the T, what luck.

The next few months, we partied and life ran its course. I was always looking to drown out my pain with drugs, booze and boosting cars. I would do anything to silence the voice and words of my mother that echoed in my head. I dragged Denel down with me, not caring what my destructive path was doing to her. Denel's family had come to their last straw with me. Her Uncle Richard asked me to go to Florida to get away from Boston and the problems I had there. Basically, it was a nice way to say, "Leave or Denel's dad is going to kill you". I was on a downward spiral and I was like a whirlwind. At that time, I had single handedly destroyed everything around me in one-way or another, maybe my mother was right. I wasn't going to amount to much and I was better off if I hadn't been born. Wow, living in my head was one of the worst things for me. What positive things I had done or what I had achieved didn't stand a chance against my mother's voice in my head constantly putting me down.

So at 19, I decided to head to Florida. Richard gave me a place to stay when I was down in Florida and had a job lined up. It sounded like maybe I had a chance to get my life together, a chance for a new start. Denel said she would move down with me once I was settled. My brother and I caught a bus to Florida and we were on the way for a fresh start. Florida was a different state, but I seemed to fall into the same ole stuff. At first I really tried, I went to work with Denel's uncle every day and stayed away from all the partying. I tried, I really did. But the partying was the only way to live with myself. I started to get back into drinking and drugs again. I wasn't working as hard as I should have been. I didn't care how it affected Denel or Richard. Then one day, Denel and I got into a fight. We fought about me not trying and she heard from someone that I had a girlfriend or something. All lies. We went our separate ways. I went off the deep end. Every time I thought I had a handle on my life, something good going on, I went and fucked it up. It didn't matter who it was that tried to help me, no matter how much they cared for me. I couldn't see it. I treated them like shit and destroyed the relationship as I continued on my way spiraling down.

I started to party hard again and got into the cocaine lifestyle. We lived in a wise guy's house from Boston. He only visited once in a great while. I would get home and he would have a kilo of cocaine spread out on the glass table. He was the king of all the bars and he got us into everywhere and anywhere. We were living like rock stars. We had no money, but we lived like the rich and famous.

My brother and I were given an opportunity to do a few runs offshore and bring in cargo to a local port, cargo being cocaine, in the keys of Florida, easy right? To a few ghetto kids from Boston it sounded magical. We would be given a cigarette boat, worth about $250,000. All we had to do was three runs at $10,000 each and on the third run we would own the boat and the debt with them would be clean. We thought long and hard. It was easy money but there was always a catch. An old timer we talked to told us the deal. He said most of the guys got caught on their third run because they would use them for bait to get other boats into Florida. We decided to back out. It was one of the smartest things we ever did. I wasn't known for doing smart things in my life. Shortly after, my brother Jimmy went back to Boston and I stayed in Florida. I couch surfed and made a few friends. It seems like even as I got older I still had the ability to make friends quickly. I was on my own and very far from home. I lived with friends on the beach of Fort Myers and partied away a good year of my life. It would always come down to how I feel and drowning the scars of my youth. Trying to get away from the monster within, or the monster I was told I was for so long. I questioned if I really was a monster or if this was another one of my mother's lies.

Joseph C Hirl

CHAPTER 4

The Move to Michigan

———————⟡⟡⟡———————

I met a girl named Jamie, while she was on Spring Break in Florida and we really hit it off. She was there on vacation with her friends from Michigan. We hung out a few times and formed a friendship. She invited me to come up to Michigan and stay for a while. She had her own place and said it would be cool to stay with her. I had never been to Michigan and I really didn't know anyone there. To be honest, I really never thought about the state of Michigan, I was still a wanted man in Boston and was on the run. I guess I thought the change would do me good, maybe I could get my life together, plus I was getting sick of Florida and the heat, so I told her yes.

I thought the change would be good and told the friends I made while I had been in Florida goodbye. I was going to try and make a new start for myself in Michigan. If I even had a clue what waited for me here in Michigan, I would have turned away and never made the trip. Not that Michigan is a bad place. It's quite beautiful to be honest. But everywhere I went, I seemed to have a dark cloud following me. I drove with Jamie back to Michigan. It was a cool ride and we had a chance to talk the whole way. Jamie was a cool girl, but she was not my type, at that time in my life I had no clue what my type even was. We were friends and we had a lot in common, like drinking and having a good time. Jamie let me crash at her place while I tried to get my life together again.

I had been so fucked up my whole life, I really didn't know too much about myself. I was 20 years old and I didn't like the person I had become. I drowned my demons out with drugs and booze. The escape was easy but trying to live in reality was hard. I missed being in Boston with my brother and sisters, it seemed like it was forever since I had seen them last. My friends from school were doing their own thing too. I heard through the grapevine that my friend Stephen had killed a man and was serving life in prison in Massachusetts. Wow, killed a man, but I guess after you have been treated like a dog and dragged through the mud your whole life, you are bound to turn on someone and he did. In my eyes, two mothers lost their kids that night, one had to bury a child and the other had to say goodbye to a child forever. Even the nicest dog will turn on its owner with enough abuse and neglect. I honestly believed Stephen just snapped.

That's the way things went for us kids that grew up poor in broken homes, we had jail and for the few lucky kids, they made it out and succeeded, but it was very rare. The odds were stacked against you right from the start, or it felt like that. So much tragedy at such a young age, we had seen the Grim Reaper's handiwork. He visited quite often and we saw it in the streets over and over again. If we were not losing our friends to the streets, we were losing them to the drugs. To heroin that flooded our streets. We looked at it like it was a part of the normal life of growing up poor and in public housing. Or maybe that was our excuse. Either way it was our reality and we had no other choice. I wished that just once I could have lived a normal life, not a rich life, just a normal life. What is normal? Is it a show we put on for other people? Or is it a coat of deception we wear to show the world how well we are doing or how rich we are? I have learned over the years, a pretty smile, or bright eyes, or a well-dressed person does not hide the pain they carry inside. It just makes the outer appearance a little softer to swallow. G towners always had each other's backs and I swear that is what kept us sane and moving forward. We were soldiers in the same fight and the same war. Stephen lost that war, I just changed battlefields.

So, we arrived in Michigan. It was a beautiful state with a lot of farmland, something I wasn't used to. I had never seen an actual cow and I remember being blown away with the sheer size of them, they were huge, I mean absolutely huge. I guess being a city boy, I missed out on the fresh air, open fields and the things people did in the country. They like to go 4 wheeling, mudding and hunting. I never experienced anyone killing something for food. I always assumed that the food came from Star Market in Quincy center or Roxie's Meat Market. I guess I missed that part of hunting our own food thing. Of course I read books where people hunted for their own food, but that was years and years ago. This state, Michigan, was a weird place to me and so very far from home and what I knew. I met a few people, but spent most of my time alone when I first moved to Lansing, Michigan.

I stuck around the house and would explore the city when Jamie went to work. At the end of the road where we lived was a river walk, and I would walk it every day and see the city. It kind of brought me back to my youth, when my brother Jimmy and I walked the river, but this was so much nicer. It was a cool city, made up of old GM plants in the process of closing down and moving. Everyone in Lansing depended on the GM factories, in one way or another. GM money was everywhere. Mostly everyone in the town was a GM worker and it was a cool little town. As the factories started to close down, it left a rampant crime wave in its wake. People had to have a way to make money and feed their families, just like every small town in America. That's where I came in. This was my thing. I was the hustle king.

I started to meet people in the area and go more places. I started hanging with a different crowd, Jamie and I started going our own ways too, different directions in life. I was meeting all the wrong people though. I would make friends quickly, but they always seemed to be the type of person that lived on the edge and took chances. Breaking the law was not anything new to me and I fell back into the same old routine. Like I said, that black cloud followed me wherever I went. I look back now and think it was self-made darkness. I now believe we create our own happiness and destiny.

One day I was at the local mall in Lansing and I was looking for something to do. I started walking through the mall and I caught a very pretty girl looking at me. I stopped and we started talking. Her name was Tracy and there was something there, some connection that you could not put into words. I told her that we could talk after she got out of work. She consumed my thoughts all day. Later that day, I met up with her and we hung out. We really hit it off. Would she see past the front I put up and see how truly messed up I was? Would she see the abuse I endured when I was little? Or see the shit I did to other people? That I was a wanted man or would she accepted the front I put up, the bullshit lies and deception.

I had to keep who I was a secret; I didn't trust anyone or anything. I have learned to keep my mouth shut about myself. Tracy and I started getting close to each other. I thought she was the right girl for me. She was pretty and she loved the crazy kid I was and the harebrained shit I did. I think if I walked into hell, she would have gone with me without asking a word. I believed she had my back.

I started to hang out with a few friends that I met in Lansing, John and Kevin. They were young and stupid like me and we fit together great or I thought. We would get drunk and drugged out, and we got into trouble, mostly stealing things to support our drinking and drug habit. If it was not glued down, we had it.

Tracy took a backseat to the drinking and drug use, but she was always there to pick up the pieces, at least as much as she could. I was good at destroying things, friendships, my life and especially relationships. I was really good at that, I was taught by the best. As hard as I was on Tracy, pushing her away, she would always have my back, I don't know why, maybe she saw something in me or thought I was worth saving, I just didn't know what she saw. This went on for months and I started to get into more trouble with the law. I thought it was funny, no one knew my real name, but Tracy, the whole time I was in Michigan, no one knew me as Joey Hirl.

I remember we were boosting a car in Eaton Rapids. The cops pulled us over and I was arrested. They asked me my name and I gave them a false name. They brought me to the police station and took my fingerprints. I kept thinking over and over again, I am busted and I am going to spend a long time in jail. I was put in this holding cell; I thought it was a closet with a window. I settled in, getting ready for whatever faced me, and I was ready. All of a sudden, my door swung open and the police officer said I was free to go. Are you kidding me I thought, you are going to release me after all I have done and all the warrants that were out there for me. Well, I grabbed my stuff and off I went. I called Tracy to come get me and we got out of dodge. I was really lucky that night.

We moved into a small camper temporarily and started our life together. We did what we wanted and lived our life the way we chose. Tracy's parents were not happy about the situation as they saw the self-destructive behavior and the downward spiral I was on. They started trying to get her to come back home and put a wedge between us. I was still breaking the law and my friends were right by my side. By this time, we had several warrants out for our arrest for crimes we committed in the last few months. It never seemed to stop us from running wild and doing what we wanted to do. We lived in a drug-induced haze. We were always high or drunk. God was never there to see us through these hard times. I was eventually arrested with my friends John and Kevin. They arrested me on a John Doe warrant, they had no idea who I was or where I came from, like a ghost of some sort. It took a few days for them to find out who I was and where I was from. I was locked down in the county and they were trying to pin a crime spree on me. It was like if they had an open case they were going to try to clean up their books with me. Tracy's mother went to the detectives and told them a lie about a fight that Tracy and I had gotten into. She made it out to be something far worse that never happened. She hoped her story would be what finally kept us apart. Her mom worked for the county and she was counting on that to get the detectives to take her word for it. As much as I had tried to keep Tracy from the worst of it, she got drug down with me. Her mother's lies ended up getting Tracy interrogated for things she was never a part of. Things got really bad and she ended up arrested. She was bailed out but the detectives kept trying to get her to admit to things that never happened, or tried to get her to back up her mom's story. They told her a bunch of lies that eventually caused her to give up on us and go her own way.

John and Kevin put everything on me and made me out to be the ringleader. I was the only one that did not talk with the detectives and they kind of wanted to hang me out to dry. I wasn't going for all that. I took the first case to a jury trial. My attorney asked the witness that supposedly talked to me, if there was anything different about the way I talked. They said "no", my attorney said that was all. He then had me take the stand and asked me to state my name and where I was born. With a big Boston accent, I said my name and where I was from. Needless to say, the jury was out for a very short time and came back with a not guilty. Mark one up for me.

The fight went like that for a year and a half. I was convicted on a few crimes and sentenced to 7 to 14 years. It was a real hard pill to swallow! I was just a confused kid, I didn't mean any harm and I never hurt anyone. Or so I thought. There were victims in my past but I didn't see it then. I was blind to the damage I caused to others because my way of treating people was shaped by abuse and manipulation. As fucked up as that is, that was my normal. In my eyes, it seemed I had been born to be a victim and as a kid I was victimized. It took me a long time to realize I wasn't a victim, but a survivor. I fought the abuse the only way I knew how and I survived.

At sentencing, before the judge sentenced me, he said, "Mr. Hirl, I don't know what the hell happened to you in your life to bring you to this point, but you are on a one way trip to self-destruction and at such a young age. I am going to sentence you to as much as I can, to save society from you. I pray you find yourself Mr. Hirl". I was so angry, I just said fuck you. I felt I was so disrespected by this judge and was not given a fair chance. I didn't have my eyes open to the fact that I created this mess. If I did not do what I did, I would have never been in front of him, in his courtroom. It felt like I was in an awful nightmare I could not escape from. I prayed, please God wake me up, I fervently prayed for any kind of intervention. However, God doesn't visit courtroom 202 in Ingham County apparently. As I waited to be transferred to state prison, I thought of my life and how badly I messed it up. I was 22 years old and created this life, my actions, my thinking and the way I was damaged as a kid. What a fucking mess!

CHAPTER 5

Off To Prison For 7 To 14

<hr>

First let me start off with, God doesn't live in Jackson State Prison, I heard his name a lot, but I never saw him there. I never saw him on the yard, I never saw him, but I never sought him out either. The only reason I was in this prison and on this block was that a detective from the small town of Charlotte had it out for me. It must have rubbed him the wrong way when he couldn't pin a few things on me, or he was just mad about the whole situation with Tracy's mom. There was something that made him mad at me, I just don't know what it was. Sometimes these small town people just don't like you because you come from the city and talk differently than they do. It always seemed to be that way. Someone, somewhere, was out to get you because they did not like you. I was so used to being hated, and not knowing why, that it had become normal for me.

When you are sentenced with the state of Michigan, you are given a number and that is your new name, I was no longer Joey Hirl, the messed up kid from G town, I was 200118, the fish (That's what they called the newcomers) and I no longer had rights, just another number amongst the thousands of other numbers. You stop and think if I was 200118, there had to be 200117 other prisoners before me who had faced what I was going to face. How many tears had hit the floor here? How many mothers who would never see their sons again. You can't let your mind run wild and think too much. I was now entering Jackson; I was entering "HELL".

As you arrive at Jackson State Prison, you walk through the doors and you are stripped of everything you own, down to your boxers, you are stripped and searched. I mean everywhere. You are asked to spread your cheeks and nothing was off limits. You are sprayed down with lice spray, sprayed down with a hose, and while you were still soaking wet, you were issued your prison blues, welcome to Jackson. Jackson State prison was an old castle looking building, bars everywhere and the inmates were housed in cells 4 tiers high, a tier ran the length of the jail house and had 30 cells on both sides.

My first night in Jackson State Prison was very difficult, I sat up all night crying, crying like a baby. I could not understand how I messed my life up so bad. How was I going to do all these years? How I ended up here in state prison by myself? I asked God why my life took such a bad turn. But God wasn't in my cell that night, he never answered me. So I sat alone, night after night, asking the same question. There were nights I considered hanging myself. I could get rid of the deep scars and the pain I was feeling. My mother was right, I was not amounting to anything. If anything, I had made my life such a mess, and I felt like I had reached the point of no return, I would never be able to get it right. I was not like the other people here, I did not belong here, I was just a screwed up kid that took a wrong road. I was not supposed to be here. Please God help me! Please.... as my voice rang silent, I was left alone with my thoughts.

I was in the same prison that Jimmy Hoffa spent his time. It was old, with deteriorating walls, the cement in the joints was crumbling away, and most of the windows were missing. The birds would fly around while you eat and they would shit everywhere, this place was covered in bird droppings. The place smelled of human urine and mold, it would take your breath away. On cold mornings, this place would be freezing, because of all the broken windows. You dare not to get out from under the blankets. You would use the heat from your breath to keep you warm, like some kind of heater system. The mice in the place were everywhere I mean everywhere. We were given a footlocker to lock up our belongings, so other inmates and the mice would not get into your personals. See when the lights went out, the mice ran wild in there, I mean they took over. You would have to tuck your blanket around your body and face to protect yourself from the creatures. You would have to sleep like a mummy with the blanket covering everything because later in the night, you would feel the mice walking around on top of your blanket and you would have to flip them off you. Kind of reminded me of living in the burnt out abandoned building in Boston, with the rats running around you. Every morning you would hear about someone that was bit during the night by mice, but no one seemed to care, we were just inmates. I learned as I went along, an inmate could have come from anywhere, there were attorneys, doctors, priests, hood thugs, Police officers and the everyday run of the mill type of guy.

I learned everyone is someone's brother, son, father, uncle and so on. Just normal people that had a bad turn on their luck or got caught up in something bad. You always question what turned them into the animals they were when they got locked up, what pushed them over the edge. I am sure they were not born that way or brought up that way. Tragedy has a funny way of making an animal out of a normal person. So many people walk around completely dead inside and never show an outward sign. You never know what might make you a man or what breaks you as a man. It's different for everybody. I believe growing up poor you don't have many choices. The choices are limited and usually lead you in one direction to keep you in poverty. When you come from money, many doors open for you and you have lots of choices. Regardless whether you're poor or have money, there are some choices that shouldn't ever be made. The outcomes for those choices are you end up in prison.

My first 2 months were in quarantine and everyone went through it. It was a time to get checked out for diseases, security level and just a general shakedown of you and your character. You had to be classified to where they would house and keep you. As I said, the officer back in the county left a remarkable note for them to watch out for me and keep me well supervised. That was so very nice of him. He was a small town detective and I was a big city boy with a Boston accent, I guess he had something to prove. As others were being classified to camps and lower levels, I would hear stories about "four block", horror stories. One day they told me to pack up, that they classed me to "four block". You only hear stories about four block, how most people go in standing up, but they come out in a body bag. The death count was crazy and you didn't want to go there, that was hell on earth. Four block, the worst block, in the worst prison in Michigan. Jackson four block was nicknamed "hell" and it was well deserved. Four block is where they kept murderers, rapist, serial killers and basically the worst offenders in the state. In addition, one messed up kid from Boston that got lost somewhere in his life. Like I said that was the worse of the worst. During the time, I was locked up in four block I was locked down for 23 hours a day. I was only allowed out in a dog size kennel with a pull up bar in it and a phone that you could only call collect from. They called that rec time and I would remember back to the day I broke all of the dogs out of the dog pound and would wonder if someone was out there that would come to save me? You would get rec time every day. It was in a dirt yard, dusty and full of predators, looking and searching for their next victim, no one could be trusted. I would always have to remember I was in four block, not the local church. I have been a victim my whole life, I refused to be a victim again.

You are given a care package, a toothbrush, a razor, pencil and a few sheets of paper. I remember my first night in four block, I broke my razor open and melted down my toothbrush handle, fashioning a knife of some sort. I needed to protect myself and I planned on holding my ground. I refused to come out of there feet first and was going to do whatever I had to make sure I walked out this place. I was going to see my family again. The first time I was in the yard a black inmate ran up behind me to test me, I pulled out my homemade knife and it made him think twice and he left me alone. The white guys saw I could hold my own and they let me in with the solid white boys. You always had someone watching out for your back and being with the white boys had its benefits for sure. You never went anywhere without a homeboy watching your back and you were watching their back, the white boys always ran in pairs. Things would always jump off in the yard or the mess hall, mainly when large groups of inmates would be placed together. The mess hall had a 4'x4' smiley face above the entry door when you walked in. They would blow the whistle when a stabbing jumped off or a fight, but it was rarely a fight with fists, these guys were killers and they wanted to hurt you as bad as they could in the short time they had. You had to hit the ground, then they would fire the first shot as a warning shot into the smiley face and the next one was a kill shot. Needless to say, I spent a lot of time on the floor in the mess hall, it was as normal as eating and just another part of the territory.

I stood my ground and was in a fight every 2 weeks defending myself. I got pretty good at fighting and defending myself. I would get into a fight and I would be locked in the hole. I knew the entire staff pretty good and they always had a room for me. I was fed nutria loaf and water. Nutria loaf was a meal ground up together into a loaf. They served that to the guys who got locked down and caused a problem. I fell into that category. See, you had to stand your ground or you would be the next person going out in a body bag and there were many body bags leaving Jackson. You mind your business and you stayed out of other people's business. This was a real eye opener. I lived in hell and for the first time, I wished to die and be done with all this pain and what I saw and lived on a daily basis. You would hear people cry all night, newbies coming in and getting raped in the shower. What a sight, but you don't dare say a word or lend a hand to help protect them. You just turned a blind eye and you minded your own business. God was blinded to what happened in four block and he was not in the shower room very often. This was hell on earth. Never in my life did I imagine there was such an awful place. Hollywood couldn't imagine such a horror and this was real life, a terrifying version of real life!

You always belonged to groups on the inside, if you were black, you hung out with the blacks and if you were white, you would only hang with the white boys. That was the way it was, you would not mix with other races, it was not allowed. In our group, you would have to be a solid white boy and hold your own. If you were asked to do something for the group, you did it without asking. There were a few times I had to stand up for the white boys while out in the yard. I guess it was a race war or a struggle as the administrator would call it. But after most struggles, you came in with wounds of some sort. I remember once I was stabbed in the side. To keep the staff from finding out, another inmate would sew you up with dental floss and a leather needle they would get from the hobby room. Very crude, but effective. I remember after one of these struggles, we were locked down and the officers would come, cell to cell, to check and see if anyone was hurt or have wounds that needed attention. This old biker cop came to my room and asked me to lift up my shirt. I lifted it half way up concealing a wound, he asked me to lift it all the way up, and he saw the wound. I thought I was in trouble, but he said, it was nice seeing you guys hold your own. I let the fight run an extra 5 minutes because you were all holding your own against double the number of the black inmates. After that, the biker cop that I nicknamed "the Sheriff" always had a little respect for me and treated me a little differently. Most people have a hood they grew up in and had homeboys from the same hood. I grew up in Boston, not too many homeboys in there from my hood. I had to stand on my own for the first two months, till the white boys knew I could hold my own, that I wasn't a rat and I was a solid white boy. They would ask to see your paperwork, your paperwork being your sentence report stating what you got sentenced for. If you were a child molester, you were treated in the worst possible way. People would spit on you and beat your ass every time they had a chance or they would make you into a sex toy to be passed around to the gay inmates. There was always a pecking order, even within the walls of Jackson. There were the prison rules and the inmates had their own rules. Sometimes those rules would crash together or the lines would be smudged. Some inmates thought they were cops and cops were thinking they wanted to act like prisoners. It was a messed up place for sure. It was a full time job staying out of their games. It was a daily struggle just to stay alive to face another day.

Death was behind every door in "four block". You truly understand "Yea, though I walk through the valley of the shadow of death, I will fear no evil" when you walk those halls. Every day you saw death, one way or another, just waiting for you to slip up and swallow you whole. You began to feel like you would never make it out of there alive, never to be heard from again. The suffering was unreal, I tell you these words, but words alone will never explain how that place was. The smell, the feel and the pure hatred that ran wild in that place. If you could imagine a hell on earth, multiply that by 100 and you might get close to "four block". It was a place right out of your worst nightmare. You walk around on high alert, never letting your guard down for a second. The people I felt bad for the most, were the mental inmates. They did not belong there and would always be taken advantage of, sexually, financially and morally. God did not protect these guys, not a chance. I always believed these were God's children. "Four block" ate them up and spit them out.

One day, I was reclassified because they found out I was too young to be in four block, four block was created for older prisoners, 25 years old and up. Not only older, but those deemed too dangerous to be in general population. Six months there and then they decided I was too young to be there. Those six months felt like 10 years of living in a nightmare I could not escape. I was reclassified to Ionia Reformatory. They called it Gladiator School because it was filled up with the youngest offenders. Young guns out to make a name for themselves and with something to prove. See you lived off your name. If people knew you would buck (fight), they would think twice about looking for trouble with you. I was starting to get the reputation of being a fighter, and was left alone for the most part. They were still murderers; rapists and the worst Michigan had to offer, just at a younger age. Ionia Reformatory was an old castle looking place, that was deteriorating from the outside and it was named right, Gladiator School. Same rules applied here, blacks hung with the blacks and the white boys ran only with white boys, you followed those rules and did not break them. Every day when I went to the yard, there was a fight of some sort, a lot of young boys with something to prove to everyone. You would gear up to go the yard, we would tape magazines around our bodies with medical tape, just in case you were stabbed. When a fight would jump off, you pulled off your socks and fill them with stones or a lock to make them into a weapon to protect yourself. The guards would say they don't get paid enough to jump into that shit and they were going to make it home that night to their families, so most fights ran their course. There always was a struggle for power between the white and the black prisoners, always. You just tried to keep to your own business and try to stay off the radar of the prison staff and other prisoners, sometimes it was hard as hell to do.

I took up a lot of my time reading old western books, they seem to take you away from your hell and transport you somewhere different. The Wild West became my escape, so far away from that 8-foot by 4 foot cell where my body was trapped. I loved drawing. I could always escape with a pencil and a piece of paper. So much pain and misery lived within those walls and I had 7 and half years to make it through. Every night you would hear people cry out to God, but God doesn't live in Ionia Reformatory and he never answered. The cries would echo down the cellblock and fade into the darkness. When you are sentenced to serve so many years, it's like a bad dream that you cannot wake up from wondering if this is real or is it a joke. I guess you get resigned to the fact that there isn't anything you can do to change what is ahead of you. No matter how much you think about it, I just wanted to be that kid again in G town, jumping creeks and hanging with my friends with no cares whatsoever. Even a nice punch in the head from my mother would be nice. The minutes turn into hours, the hours turn into days, the days turn into years and then one day you will be free, if you make it that far. You don't have Christmas, you don't have birthdays and you don't have any holidays at all. They all blend together into just another day. I guess you could give up and end your life, which a lot of people did. They just couldn't face another day away from their family, girlfriends and friends. Or you become strong and turn into the animals that fit into this hell, be strong and be a gladiator. I chose to be strong and do what was in front of me. I never thought I would ever make it to the end of my sentence, no way. I thought I would have been killed or I would just get so sick of it and hang myself. It's a real eye opener. I guess you never know how strong you are, till being strong is all you have. Was I going to be an animal when this was all done, worse than I ever had been?

After a year of Gladiator School, I got reclassified to a lower security facility. I was no longer in supermax, I was just in max. I got moved over to Muskegon and served the next few years there. I made a pen pal at this time. A friend of mine's girlfriend set it up. She thought we would hit it off. I wrote her a letter, she wrote back and we seemed to connect. We started writing to each other all the time, she made my time go a little easier and she always made me smile. She made me feel things that I felt were long dead inside of me. We would write all the time and I would call her every now and then. She seemed like a really nice person and through our letters, we got to know one another on a whole different level. Her name was Carole. After a while Carole decided she would come visit me and I was really nervous. I wasn't used to getting visits, because my family lived so far away. The first time Carole came to visit, she was more beautiful than I ever had imagined. I was so nervous and I was stumbling over my words. I wasn't used to being around girls, just hardcore inmates. Our visit went off without a hitch and she saw something in me that was worth investing her time in. I mean she was beautiful and could have any guy out in the free world, why would she invest her time in me.

Things were good between us and I started to stay out of trouble more and more, that way I could get her visits. I really enjoyed spending time with her. We started talking about our future and what kind of plans we were going to make. I asked her if she would consider marrying me and to my surprise she said yes. I guess I just didn't want to lose her, I truly loved her and she loved me. You see, when you write to someone on a regular basis, you truly get to know them on so many levels, because we talked about everything and anything. We knew each other so well.

We made plans together and being married would make it that much closer to reality. So, we got married while I was incarcerated. After we got married, it was very weird because we had to go our own ways. She returned home and I had to return to my cell. Not the way you plan your honeymoon night, but thankfully we were married now. So at the age of 28 I was married and became a stepdad to Carole's 7-year-old daughter Rachell.

In 1994, I got reclassified to Kinross and it was up over the bridge of Michigan, the Upper Peninsula. I spent my remaining years in Kinross. Kinross was a very laid-back prison. There was a lot of stuff to do and to keep the inmates busy, in positive ways. I joined the Jaycees and did fundraisers. I enjoyed raising money for the "Make A Wish Foundation". I studied in school and I got my GED, and I started college classes. I played a lot of sports and lifted weights every day. I started to get into shape, both mind and body. Kinross was so very far away from the Jackson four block and Ionia Reformatory, but I would never forget those places. I had seen way too much death, pain, suffering and hurt at the devil's playground.

After seven and a half years, I went in front of the parole board and was granted parole, but it wasn't that easy. After being granted parole, little did I know there was a hold on me from Massachusetts. Seems like I owed a little more time to them that I never finished and I had honestly just forgotten about it. I thought, just another heartbreaker in my life. I was released on parole and like Boston promised, they were there to get me. Carole was happy that I had received parole, then I had to break the bad news that Massachusetts was going to pick me up and take me back to Boston to finish some time I forgot I had. I thought things with her were done; she just made it to the end of her rope. It is very hard to have a relationship with someone behind walls and I understood it, I do not know if I could have done it if the roles were reversed.

I traveled back to Boston in the back of a van for three days, getting out only to use the restroom in handcuffs and spending nights in county jails along the way. After 3 days, I made it back to Massachusetts. After being there for 60 days, Boston released me and I was finally free. They called my name around 6 o'clock and told me to pack it up. As the heavy steel door opened, I was free. I started to run, I didn't want them to think they made a mistake and take me back, over seven years locked up and I was finally free. Freedom never tasted so good. My first breath of fresh air as a free man, I made it out the other end and I was finally free. I will never take this road again, never again. I paid my dues and maybe a little more.

CHAPTER 6

Freedom at last

fter being released for the first time in over seven years, I finally knew what freedom tasted like and I loved it. I was 30 and literally starting my life over again. I really didn't know anyone in my family anymore. They were complete strangers to me, the last time I had seen anyone was over 8 years ago. I didn't even know what they looked like anymore, my brother had kids now and they didn't know me or what I just went through. My sister Cindi had kids and was married now, they didn't know me either. My mother was married now. I was never at the wedding. As I looked at the wedding pictures, everyone was there, smiling and having a good time, except me, I was left out of everything. I thought to myself, did you think of me even a little during these times or was I just a lost thought. Did they ever pray for me while I was going through hell and fighting for my life? If they did, was God even going to listen? I was locked away in Michigan. I came home to strangers. What a feeling, to be released out to a world that kept turning while your world sat at a complete standstill. I was stuck in time, 7 years ago, while everything and everyone moved forward. I stayed at a standstill, nothing gained and everything lost. If anything, I had turned into an animal in the last 7 years, I knew survival of the fittest and prison rules. The world doesn't play by four block rules or prison code, or all the bullshit that comes along with it.

How do I blend the two worlds together? I was a stranger in my own family, a stranger to my brother and his kids. A stranger to my sister Cindi, her husband

and her kids. I was an outsider. I didn't exist for so long in my family's eyes and in their lives. I missed so much and accomplished so little. As I started to get to know my family again and their kids, I decided I was going to get my life right and do the right things for the first time in my life.

I really wanted to live a normal life, I wanted a family of my own, I wanted to work, hold a job and even drive a car legally. I wanted to have a life I could be proud of. I had to first stay at my mother's house once again and I was afraid what that would be like, I was now a different man. Had she changed or was she going to be the same person I left behind so many years ago. I guess I had no other choice and I was a grown man now, I could protect myself and I did not allow anybody to disrespect me in any way, prison taught me that. I just spent the last few years with the worst of the worst, how bad could she be.

I guess time mellowed her out a bit or it seemed like it to me, on the surface that is. She was a different lady and I noticed the change immediately. I think she also knew I was a different man and would not stand for the abuse or words she said so freely when I was a child, abuse that cut me deeply and haunted me in my life. That taught me to be the animal I turned out to be, devoid of feeling human, no sense of empathy or how to love and be loved. I turned out the way she always said I would, that I would not amount to anything. Now, I was given a second chance to get my life together, to be something and prove her wrong. I noticed her moods would change and I think it was the pills she was taking, I think they were painkillers of some sort. I immediately got a job with an asphalt company sealing driveways. It was a shitty job, but it was a job and I was making legal money for the first time in my life. I showed up every day on time and ready to work.

Carole and I started talking again after a few months. Seems she wasn't too mad at me anymore, once she knew I was telling her the truth and Boston messed up. She wanted to come out to Massachusetts to see me and start a life with me. The last time I talked with her, we left it on bad terms, so this made me happy. Carole came out to visit me in Massachusetts. I truly loved her and wanted her to come out and stay with me. We were going to stay at my mother's house until we got on our feet. We both worked full time jobs trying to get enough money to get our own place. But my mother's old ways surfaced again and this time I would not take her abuse! I finally told her how I felt. We had a major blow out, Carole and I left.

I held my ground and we were now homeless. We ended up getting our own place and living on our own. It was nice for once, to have our place where we could do as we pleased. It was our home and we started living life together for the first time. After getting off parole, we decided to move back to Michigan, where Carole's family lived, and get away from Boston all together and the high cost of living there. We rented a U-Haul and moved back to Michigan, Carole, Rachell (My stepdaughter) and myself.

We moved to the small town of Kalkaska and I applied for a job working on an oilrig. I was warned how tough it was going to be and I thought I was just a little bit tougher. I got hired to work on a work over rig, a work over rig worked on oil wells that had problems, blocked off, broken pipes or environmental plug-ins. After the oil was pulled from the ground, we would pull the entire pipe up from the ground and plug the hole for good. It was hard work, but I picked up on it quickly and did well. We would work in 10 below zero temperatures round tripping pipe, I was always cold, but the money was good.

Northern Michigan was very beautiful, even with the snow on the ground. We lived in the Snow Belt and I was not used to snow like that. The amount of snow northern Michigan gets is completely crazy. You could be driving and hit a wall of snow. When I say you hit a wall of snow, I mean that literally. The weather can be sunny and calm one second and the next second you see a wall of snow coming at you. Beautiful but crazy at the same time sunshine behind you, and a wall of white ahead of you. There was a line on the ground, where the snow would start and you just drive into it.

I stayed working on the oilrig for a little while and we decided to move down state to the city of Big Rapids and buy a house there. Carole was from the area and her parents lived there as well. We found a house and we moved in. It was a great neighborhood and I got a job working full time at a local shoe company making boots. Our first child was born in 1996, Taylor Alicia Marie Hirl, yes I named my daughter after my mother. Maybe in some way I thought I would finally gain her approval. Our son Joseph Carl Hirl II followed in 1999. I guess at this point in my life, I was all right with my mother and wanted her to love me. I would later learn, that the people who abuse you while you were growing up and never had their approval, for some reason, you still look for their approval later in life. I wanted my mother's approval so bad. She would take trips to my home from Boston, sometimes they were good, but then other times she tried to be abusive to my kids and I would stand up to her and there would be a massive fight. I would always stand my ground; my kids would never feel the lash of her words. That was that.

I continued to look for her approval and her love. By this time in life, my mother was addicted to painkillers and spent most of her time chasing them down. She would come in from Boston, and within hours she would find a connection. See pain pill abusers always seem to find one another, as if they had a hotline to wherever you go to hook up with others like you. She was getting old and frail, but she still had a mouth on her, she was never happy with anyone. If you took her out for dinner, the staff was the worst, the food was cold and she could never be satisfied. I don't think she ever had a happy minute in her life especially since she was always so busy with the negative aspects of life.

I learned to love my mother the way she was and I had a small amount of respect for the woman she had become, a small amount. I loved her and I believed she had love for me. My kids loved her, Rachell, Taylor and Joseph. My mother was proud of all of them. I guess she did change somewhat. I guess time wore her down, or something softened her heart. I don't know for sure. I guess I really enjoyed having her around for the first time in my life. I never forgot her words, but I guess I spent my whole life, up until this point hating her. It was time to try and love her for once and let go of the hatred I held inside for so long.

My father passed away in 2002 of heart failure. We never really reconciled and had very few moments of contact before his death. I guess he never had time for his children and kept to himself for the most part. I attended his funeral and I will never forget it. As I walked into the funeral home, my two uncles were at the door welcoming people. They asked if they could help me. I felt like I was a complete stranger and out of place there. I just said no and carried on. As I passed them, I could hear one of them say to the other, "that's Joey, he looks just like his father". What a feeling to know that my father's side of the family didn't even know me, didn't even know who I was. But they saw the resemblance and knew my name.

After I knelt at my father's coffin, I put pictures of my children under his pillow to bury with him. See, my father never met my children and they never knew he even existed. Later in life my kids would ask about him, but what could I tell them, I didn't know much about the man he was. My father was a ghost for most of my life. I saw my uncle approach my grandmother and whisper in her ear as he pointed in my direction. As my grandmother approached me, she tried to give me a hug. I told her it was not necessary and that she should have been hugging me when I was 4 or 5, that's when I needed the hugs. I was no longer a child; I was now a grown man and walked right past her. I don't know if that was the right thing to do, but I was very angry. I carried a lot of resentment towards the whole family. In a way, they had their own part in creating the monster that stood in front of them.

I did get a good laugh at my father's wake. See my father spent the last year of his life in a nursing home on a heart monitor. My brother and I had a friend Dino, who came to show his respect. As Dino entered the funeral home, my uncle asked him if he could help him. As I eavesdropped, Dino stated he was here for Jimmy, meaning my brother, but they thought he was there for my father. They asked him how he knew Jimmy, Dino stated he played softball with Jimmy and how they just won the championship last week. As Dino walked away, my uncles were left standing there with an odd-looking frown on their face. It was if they were trying to figure out how my father had been playing softball a week ago.

Things were good in my life. I always held on to the tough guy image, I guess I had lived it for so long that's all I knew. I joined an outlaw bike club. I was vice president and I started to get into it pretty deep. I loved the brotherhood. I loved my brothers and the way we had each other's back. I was trained for this through my many years in jail. I mean I fit right in, brotherhood, Harleys, the drinking and drugs, shit this is what I had been looking for all my life. They never judged me, I felt like I fit in. I eventually had to walk away because the drugs were gaining too much control on my life again. I had an old biker friend talk some sense into me, he told me what I was headed for and what the outcome would be of me continuing to ride with these guys. I was nothing but a federal number and a federal case file on me. I think I already had one at that point, at least the federal number.

By this time in my life, I had been out of trouble for over 20 years, yes 20 years trouble free. I guess after you have been through such hell, especially when that hell is being in the Michigan prison system, you never want to go back, never. Having a wife, kids and a normal life saved me.

But I always had to have control over everything in my life, because I believed only in myself. I would try to attend church, but I never got anything out of the message. I guess when you just believe in yourself for so long, it's hard to trust someone else to help you in your life. Plus I just didn't believe in a God. I have been through too much and I have seen too many things to believe this loving God existed anywhere. The world was messed up and people sucked. How could there be a God, right? I looked at other people in church as sheep that were brainwashed. They sit here every Sunday and worship some person's idea of who God is, made up in some person's head so long ago. Why couldn't the world see past this charade? It left me mad and I felt like I could see the truth behind this God thing. Like in the Wizard of Oz when Dorothy looks behind the curtain and sees that the wizard isn't this all mighty presence. I just thought it was a way to separate you from your money and have control over your life. Just like sheep herded together. Every Sunday returning to worship something or someone that just did not exist, period! How can this many people be blind to the suffering in the world today? Were things that bad that we just needed something, anything to believe in?

I continued to live in Big Rapids. I started working for a rental company. Things were good and I stayed with the rental company for 13 years. After 13 years it got kind of old and it was time to move on to bigger and better things. I decided to start a business of my own. I would go on to start a painting and power washing business. I loved to paint and I wanted to own my own business. The first year I did very well and business started picking up. Over the years it provided a good life for my family. I felt good, but I started to gain weight and decided I would quit smoking and try exercising. I quit smoking for a year. I started riding my bike and walking at night. I would walk with my son Joseph and my nephew Brendan, I enjoyed the time with them and it gave me a chance to catch up on what was going on with Joseph.

CHAPTER 7

July 2, 2014

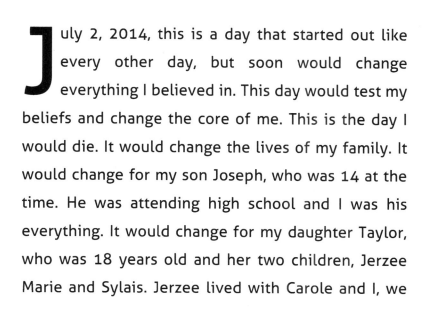

July 2, 2014, this is a day that started out like every other day, but soon would change everything I believed in. This day would test my beliefs and change the core of me. This is the day I would die. It would change the lives of my family. It would change for my son Joseph, who was 14 at the time. He was attending high school and I was his everything. It would change for my daughter Taylor, who was 18 years old and her two children, Jerzee Marie and Sylais. Jerzee lived with Carole and I, we had custody of her and she looked at me like a father figure. This little girl always made me smile with happiness. She had a rough start in her life. I wanted her to have a good life, where she knew people cared about her and loved her. Carole, most of all, would have her life, as she knew it, ripped from her. Her life would never be the same, and the journey she faced was going to be a hard and long road. Carole was alone and making decisions that would affect the rest of my life, if I still had a life. My life was in her hands. Her decisions would affect every part of my being. We had never talked about something like this happening. There was no plan, nothing in place about medical decisions and no will. She was completely on her own. I no longer had control over anything and my life was in other people's hands, not my own.

See, this day started out like every other day. I went to work just like any typical day without knowing it was going to be anything but typical. I worked all day and came home. It was a long hard day. Had dinner with my family and decided to go out for a bike ride with my son Joseph and my nephew Brendan. We talked about what had happened during the day, normal stuff like we always do. After the ride, I took a shower and I lay down in bed to watch some TV, like I did every night before I went to sleep. Everything seemed normal, but that would soon change. I started to get a few chest pains and I brushed them off as getting old and working hard that day. After a few more chest pains, I started to feel really uncomfortable, the pain was like a building pressure, like something squeezing or pressing on my chest. I never felt that before. I started to get nervous; I could feel my heartbeat throb in my chest, beating rapidly.

I began to sweat, I started to feel sick and I just didn't feel right, something just was not right. Damn, what was happening to me? Carole was visiting friends across the street. She would visit and have coffee with the neighbors every so often. I got into my work van and pulled over to the neighbor's house. I asked her if she wanted to go to the hospital with me. I told her that I was not feeling too good and I thought something was really wrong. I try to avoid the hospital as much as I can, for one, we did not have health insurance and the other, well I'm a man and I think everything will pass. She jumped in my van and we headed to the hospital. Carole could see something in my face or eyes that things were not right. Halfway there I told her I was going to stop at a local store to get some aspirin and go home. I told her we couldn't afford a hospital bill without insurance and this would pass, but she talked me into letting her drive and she would get us to the hospital. En route to the hospital, Carole said I lost consciousness and I suddenly slumped over on the seat of the van. With my survival on the line, she continued on to the hospital. She said that she was afraid I was gone for good. As she pulled up to the hospital, she saw a doctor standing outside in the ambulance bay talking on his phone, it was rare to see a doctor outside. The man standing outside was Dr. Morris, a man that would have such an impact on my life and if I would live or die, he would decide that fate. He was a humble man by all means, soft spoken, but his words carry meaning, if you know what I mean.

Carole pulled up to the doctor and said "my husband is dying" and he said, "Everyone says that". As he peered into the van, he could see me blue and slumped on the seat. He immediately went into the emergency room and got help. The emergency room staff came running out and they pulled my lifeless body from the van and got me onto a gurney. This task was not easy by any means, I am a big man, I am and 6' 5" and weigh just over 300 pounds. They got me into the trauma room, and started working on me. The doctors and nurses took turns doing CPR. Every time they would get a pulse on me, they would lose it. This happened repeatedly. Dr. Morris teaches CPR and he said, "When it is done right, it saves lives". I was lucky that night, I had all the right people in the right places. You see, in 20 years of being a doctor, Dr. Morris had only stepped out of the emergency room, a few times to use his phone and to be there when I pulled up had to be an act of God. It had to be some kind of divine intervention. Wait. Did I say an act of whom? They told Carole later that if she had come through the regular emergency room entrance to get help, I would have died where I was. That's how precious time was for me. For Dr. Morris to be where he was that night was a pure miracle in every sense of the word.

Every time they got a pulse, I would bottom right out again. The Dr. was going to pronounce me dead twice and he said every time he was ready to call it, my heart would shudder and they would start CPR again. He said that if I had the will to fight then he was going to fight too. He later asked me if I could hear him getting ready to call the time of death. I flatlined for 57 minutes, that's a lifetime when they are working on you to bring you back, it's unheard of, it just does not happen. Outside there was a thunderstorm carrying on, thunder roaring and the lightning cracked, while I was fighting for my life. It's as if the heavens knew a battle was going on inside the ER that night and there was a battle raging outside just as strong.

Carole was in the waiting room and she knew, as the time ticked away it was bad, time was precious. She had been in the medical field and knew there was something very wrong with me. There was way too much time that had passed and the grim reminder of people being worked on like that did not have a positive outcome. As time went by and the medical team worked on me, they would bring me back just to lose me again. It was a continued fight the whole time.

The storm was still raging outside, while the ER team inside worked on getting me stable. When they finally got me stable, shaky, but stable enough to move me to the heart hospital where I immediately needed to be, where I needed to be an hour ago. The ER team called for a Med-flight helicopter to come pick me up. Because in my condition, that was the only way I would make it to the heart hospital in Grand Rapids, by air, a 60-minute car ride without the appropriate medical support would kill me. Med-flight said they could not lift off because of the raging thunderstorm that was going on that night, kind of like the heavens were fighting over me. They called another Med-flight from down state, they started to come to get me, but got within 14 minutes of the hospital and had to abort the mission because of the storm, the storm was just too bad that night.

Once again, the odds were stacked against me. Had I made it this far just to die because I could not make it to the heart center and the whole effort of the ER team would be washed away? I don't think anyone that night, Doctors, nurses or bystanders thought I had any kind of chance for survival. It was a grim outlook. Life was unfair and once again, I was thrown into survival mode. The Dr. made a quick decision, he decided that they would drop my temp, to slow everything down in my body and send me by ambulance to the heart center. Not that he thought I would make it. Once you die, your body starts to shut down and organs start to die off, it's such a mess and some damage is not repairable. The odds were stacked against me for sure.

The doctor went out and talked with my family. He told them the grim news, that I had a massive heart attack and that I was a very, very sick man. I was stable and they decided to send me down to the heart hospital by ambulance, because the Med-flights just could not transport me with the raging storm that was outside. The doctor let them know my chances of making it to the heart hospital were very slim and if they want to say goodbye to me, this would be the time to do so. Carole had to get the kids up there to tell them the grim news, that their father was going to die and they needed to say goodbye to him. Joseph was told the news, broke down, and ran out of the hospital, crying and confused. As I write this, I have tears running down my face and it weighs heavy on my heart that my 14 year old son had to say what he and everybody else thought was goodbye to his father forever. This was so unfair, so very unfair. He would never see me again or share how his day went or anything, just heartbreaking. Carole would have to call my brothers and sisters and let them know the same thing, your brother is on his deathbed and if you wanted to say goodbye this would be the time. How can my life end like this? Please God, help me, please help me.

I fought so hard in my life, I was a fighter, and I survived things that most people would have died from. I was the tough guy, I didn't take shit from no one, and I was bulletproof and untouchable. As my temp was lowered, and the doctor was getting ready for me to be transported to the Grand Rapids Heart Hospital, I heard the phrase "WIDOW MAKER". Because what I just had was called a widow maker and one of the most serious heart attacks. I never seem to do anything small, yes a widow maker. My family said their goodbyes through tears, knowing this would be the last time they would see me alive. The doctor made it known that it was a very slim chance that I would make it to the Grand Rapids Heart Hospital. With heavy hearts, they said their goodbyes.

The Dr said it was in God's hands and it would take a miracle if I made it to the heart hospital. Wait did he just say it was in God's hands, Hopefully not the same God that wasn't there in Dorchester, or G town, or DYS or even Jackson, we were not counting on that God, were we??? Oh boy, I think we were, was God going to be another no show? Please God, save me.

My brother in law showed up to comfort his sister and stand by her side. He is a good man and the protector of the family. He would make sure Carole made it down to the heart hospital, probably before the ambulance. I was prepped for the ride ahead of me and they loaded me into the ambulance after a fight for my life that was fought long and hard. The ER staff that worked on me for hours, to give me back life, just to see it fade away again and again, all watched me get loaded into the ambulance, knowing that I didn't have a chance in hell to make it out of this alive. They saw this story play out way too many times and knew the outcome. The odds were stacked against me I would need a miracle.

Too much time had lapsed, no blood to my brain, no oxygen, there would be damage beyond what the doctors or God could repair. I was doomed. I guess I needed a miracle and God to step in. I was loaded up and the ER nurse named Carol Anne, a friend and former coworker of my wife's, was my attending nurse the whole way down to the Grand Rapids Heart Center. Carol Anne is an angel and took that ride with me. As we arrived at the heart center, yes I made it, by the grace of God, I made it. I had beaten the odds, but this was only the beginning of my long road to recovery. Maybe God was watching. Just maybe.

As I was brought into the heart center, they asked Carol Anne "why would you work on him for so long when there wasn't a chance he would get any better" and "there would be damage beyond repair and that they would have called me dead after 10 minutes". Wow, I didn't have a chance. She responded by saying "how can you put a time on a life". She did the right thing. I was alive, because of the entire ER team's grit and determination.

That night was a bumpy night for me, I was sent right to the catheter lab and they decided that I had two main blockages in the main arteries to my heart. This was the worst of the worst and I would have to have four stents put in to remove the blockages and restore proper cardiac function. They went through an artery in my groin, up into my heart, cleared the blockage and installed the four stents. I was placed in the ICU and on life support. I had an IV pole that one nurse was dedicated to managing. I had lines running in and out of every vein in my body and I had a machine breathing for me. There was a machine that did everything for me, the full works. I was being kept alive by machines. I was in a bad way and a very sick man to say the least.

After a few days the doctors tried to take me off life support, it was short lived and I would always crash. My heart would beat around 200 times a minute and flutter out of control. I had to be put back on life support. Someone was always with me. I was never left alone the whole 15 days I was in ICU. Thanks to my wife, sister, my friend Jason and his wife Cindy, Zoey (their daughter) and my family. My sister Cindi flew in from Boston, where she was vacationing on Cape Cod. She needed to be by my side. See, I lost my mother 2 years and 2 days to the date that I died. Yes isn't that ironic, 2 years and 2 days. My sister Cindi happened to be in Massachusetts, again, vacationing when my mom died. My mother later in life just loved Christmas in July, it was a time she looked forward to all year long. The grandkids and her kids would come to her house and celebrate. So, every July 4th, we would gather at her home and celebrate Christmas in July. It's a funny thing she died on July 4th, one of her happiest days of the year.

The doctors would go through these attempts to wean me off life support only to crash out again. My heart was beating 200 times a minute and the doctor told my wife that my heart would not handle that for too much longer, you can only run a heart at that speed for so long before it gives out totally. Two steps forward and three steps back. They decided that I needed an ablation, that they would burn a line across my heart to stop the heart from fluttering, the top part of my heart and the bottom were not in sync. They were out of rhythm. They did the ablation and it stopped the flutter. Now I had an irregular heartbeat, commonly called a-fib, which is where the heart beats at an off rhythm. The ablation would consist of shocking your heart until it got back into normal rhythm; I know it sounds easy; you just shoot a bolt of electricity into your heart. Cardiac ablation is a procedure that scars or destroys tissue in your heart that's allowing an incorrect electrical signal to cause abnormal heartbeats... It's kind of crazy to think about it today, my heart has been shocked, stints put in, a line burned across it, more tissue burned and shocked again.

The days went by and I held my own, but not really, they had machines doing the work for me. The doctors kept saying the outlook would be grim, "don't expect much more than a vegetable when he wakes up" and that I would not talk, walk or anything. That I would need long term care, maybe a nursing home or something. Carole had to face these possibilities on her own. We had never talked about a medical emergency like this. We had no plan. I had one Dr. that totally believed that I would come out of this experience and be fine, he told this to my wife Carole all the time. The times they would take me off life support, the Dr. would be there with a big smile and a thumb up, like an angel. My family kept the faith and watched over me every day and night. My wife made sure I was being washed and received the basic care I needed.

Finally, I was taken off life support and remained stable. I remember waking up, and I saw my wife there, I was confused. The first thing I told my wife was I had seen my mother and she said, "Joey you need to go back, it's not your time." She explained that I died and what had gone on for the last few weeks. As

I rested I started to remember what happened, I remember looking down at my body on the table of the ER, with people working on me, sitting on me, giving me CPR, It was like I was right there, looking down and watching myself lose my life and regain it, I saw the nurses taking turns, I could see my wife in the waiting room, looking worried and nervous, praying in the little church right outside the ER. This was crazy. How could I see that when I was dead? Lifeless. Could this be a dream, no way, it was too real for any dream. I was scared, this was a wake-up call to my faith.

CHAPTER 8

The Awakening

hat lies beyond death? This seems to be one of the greatest questions in the world. What happens when we die? First thing I remember there was a bright light made up of a million bright lights, of all colors combined into one bright light and I knew it was God watching over me. A light so bright that it consumed everything, a warm and comforting glow that engulfed me. The bright soothing light drowned out everything around it, it was blinding and comforting. I could feel the fear, the concerns of life, the pain wash away from my soul, like taking off an old heavy coat after a long winter outside. It made me feel lighter than air. I was engulfed in the love of the light. It was like I knew everything, the meaning of life, why I was born, why I was given the hard life I had, why I had to go through what I went through and it was finally going to be all right. It was like a bolt of electricity shot through my soul and I was given the understanding of life and our purpose here on earth. No words were ever spoken, but you just were enlightened with the knowledge of what was going on and what you were about to face without a single word, I was all right, finally I was all right. I could feel my soul leave my lifeless body, as I crossed over and floated above the operating table and there was calm. I wasn't afraid. I felt comfort and finally at peace. Like it was perfectly normal to be floating above my body, nothing strange about it at all. It all seemed so normal, like I was watching someone else lying there on the table. I was floating above myself, so how could I not be there and here.

As I hovered above my lifeless body, I could watch the ER team work on me. Hit me with electricity. I got hit 13 times that night with defibrillator paddles. When I finally came through weeks later, I had burn marks on my chest, that's how many times they hit me. I could see a little red headed nurse on top of me doing chest compressions. I saw them taking turns, each person doing their job. I was not nervous. Every time they lost me, it was all right either way. I could see the room I was in, so clean and sterile, so bright and mass chaos as I watched. I could see it all and I was all right with it. I could see my wife in the waiting room, scared, worried and confused. Why did she look like that? I thought I was alright. I was safe. I did not realize that I had died. The doctor would later ask me if I knew he was going to call my time of death twice. He said that every time he got ready to call the time of death, my heart would flutter, like I knew what was coming next. It's only human to fight to stay alive and win the ultimate victory over death, right.

I did not feel the pain anymore, I wasn't hurting and I was at peace. Peaceful for once in my life, my worries washed away, I had true inner peace. I have had ADHD my whole life, my ADHD, was cleared, I could think straight, no racing thoughts, just calmness and understanding that everything was going to be alright. I was truly at peace for once in my life.

Everyone says you see the bright light, I thought that was a made up experience. I did not believe in this, life after death, come on, this was not true, but there it was, right in front of me. You do, you really do see the light. I also saw a million lights of all colors combined into one bright golden white light, almost like a tunnel. The closer you got, the more you could feel comfort and complete love wash over you. The light became even brighter and I knew it was heaven. It was like I belonged here, for once I felt as if I belonged somewhere and it was pulling me closer. I felt a presence with me, a guardian angel, and an angel so beautiful it brought me to tears. There were no words that were spoken. It was like we talked without saying a word. The guardian angel was with me the whole time, never leaving my side, guiding me and showing me the right trail to stay on. As we got closer to the light, I could see faces of people I knew. Relatives that passed before me- my father, and my grandmother's faces flashed in front of me, welcoming me, happy and at peace. Illnesses that once held them down were all gone. I could hear their words without them saying a thing or moving their lips. They were there to welcome me, but why? This is so unbelievable and so beautiful. I could only dream of something this beautiful, but here it was in front of me. The feeling of love engulfed me totally.

Going through the light was beautiful, I crossed over, the peace and beauty is beyond words. As my eyes adjusted I could see clearly, everything was in high definition. Colors so pure and bright, dazzling your eyes but not causing you to squint due to the brightness, you could still look at them directly and pick out individual colors. Brighter and more sparkling than any jewel you'd ever seen on earth. Rolling green hills in the distance, a sky bluer than anything you've ever seen. A gentle breeze that filled you with a peace and calm you'd never felt before. Everything lush and simple all at once. I think about it today and I get goose bumps and a chill that runs down my spine. How could this exist, I didn't believe in this, I did not believe in God. Was I wrong all these years? Life as we know it has no comparison to this, nothing.

I was brought to be judged. I started to see my life flash in front of me, like a picture show. My life was being reviewed, oh boy, I wasn't prepared for what I was shown.

First I was shown my family, the joy they brought into my life and also the sadness I caused. I saw the birth of my children. I saw the times I was there to comfort them in their times of need. How I taught them to do things, like ride a bike or their first day of school. But then I was shown them crying by my bedside, crying cause they lost their dad and would never have him again. I thought of all the things I should have told them but never did. Like how proud I was of them and what they meant to me. How they changed my life for the better and how much I loved them, unconditionally. How I would have never been a better person without them in my life and how I would truly miss them with all my heart. Things I should have told them every day, things that don't cost a penny, but could change another person's life forever. Will my children know how much they were loved and how they made me a better person? How they were my everything in life, that they were my life and they made it complete. Will they know?

I saw the day I met my wife and the smiles we shared, the times we made each other laugh, her giving birth to my children, but then I saw her crying at the hospital. Sitting by my bedside, thinking she would never see me again or hold my hand. No one had ever prepared her for my death. We never had a discussion on a living will or medical decisions. I realized it was something that should have been discussed. As I watched her crying I thought, I should have told you how much you meant to me, I should have told you how much I loved you every day and every night before bed. I shouldn't ever have gone to bed mad about something stupid. It never seems like we tell the people in our lives how much they mean to us, then it's too late and the chance is gone. Will she ever know?

I saw my brother and sister. The times we covered for each other as kids. The happy times we spent just hanging out. The times my brother and I hung out when we walked the river, the nights we talked into our pillows, when he helped me ride my bike, and just being a big brother. I also saw him at home worrying about me crying, confused and asking God to save me. I could see him getting drunk and thinking how unfair life was. He just wanted his little brother back. I saw my sister Cindi as a little girl, my baby sister. I saw all the times she risked a beating to have my back because she loved her big brother. I saw her fighting back tears as she prepared to get on a flight to Michigan to have my back once again, maybe for the last time. The years lost to my incarceration. Watching those lives I wasn't a part of. Realizing how much I loved them.

I saw my childhood memories. Hanging out with Stephen, the times we would walk to Lester's. The day I let the dogs loose from the pound. Days filled with sunshine and happiness in just being a kid outside with my friends doing things that kids do. Days I took for granted and didn't appreciate. I saw the moments the darkness that became my childhood started. All those nights living in basements, alone, scared and hiding from the cops and my mother. I was shown God watching over me, protecting me, but I was too blind to see it. I had pleaded and begged for an answer, an intervention, some sign that he was real and listening. But there was no bolt from the sky, no miracles. There was nothing that I could point to know that he was there or listening or even cared. So I just blocked him out of my life altogether. Just like I blocked out everyone else that I thought had turned his or her backs on me. Could I have been wrong all those years when I didn't get the answer I was looking for when I cried out. I was mad at God because I never got the answer I wanted when I wanted it. Therefore he just did not exist. Boy was I wrong.

I was then shown what the other half of the coin looked like. I was plunged into darkness. It was pitch black, blacker than black. I felt my guardian angel leave my side. I was left all alone. The fear washed over my body. I mean, earth-shaking fear, that chilled you right to the bone and left you shaking like you just went outside in the dead of winter without a coat. It was just a void and you felt all these eyes on you, watching you and examining you through the imperceptible darkness. But I could not see a thing through the utter darkness. It was like when you can feel someone looking at you, but this feeling was even worse. It felt like a million eyes on you, piercing through your whole being, tearing through every layer that made you who you were. The fear gripped me and I was afraid. I wanted this to stop and be done with all of this.

I felt sick to my stomach, a gut wrenching sickness I had never felt before. Just beyond any words could describe. I felt hopeless and confused again, I felt despair and loneliness like no other time in my life. The smell was like nothing you had ever smelled, rotten, sulfur, burning hair just a vile smell. I could hear the screams of others echo through my head, like a long song of screams. Just going on and on and on, echoing in your head. I was reminded of the shame I felt being abused as a child by my mother, the pain of her physical and mental abuse. Her words that always had cut through me, scarred me as a child, and followed me into my adult years ringing in my head. Making me feel worthless. The harsh words she spoke about me never amounting to anything. Those feelings rushed right in and consumed me. The loveless childhood I had, every time I cowered in a corner, every time I was alone and every time I felt unwanted, it consumed every fiber in me and those feelings were fresh and raw again.

I saw the past relationships that I ruined with the people who truly loved me, cared about me despite all the bullshit. I never gave a second thought about their feelings. Would they ever know how I felt, how I truly felt inside? I tasted every tear that had been cried over me until my mouth was full of salt. I felt the heartbreak I had caused strike me like a knife in the chest, over and over. Every feeling they felt, I now felt. Their confusion that came from me pushing them away for no real reason. My incredible anger at them when I realized they weren't there anymore. The sadness when I treated them poorly. The pain from every lie or harsh word I spoke to them. The grief and anguish over a child lost and the complications that caused long term. I felt all of it. There was no way to stop it. I couldn't close my eyes or turn away. I couldn't walk out and avoid their sorrow. It was overwhelming. I saw how the pain and heartache that my actions caused, my words and the way I treated them stayed with them years later. I never knew or cared how badly I had hurt them, but boy did I now. I was very selfish, self-centered and consumed by all the wrong things. I was blinded and could not see the truth.

The crimes I committed against other people, morally and physically. The things I did in the dark that were done because of a code. I saw faces flash before me, the looks of fear and dread as they sensed what was coming. The cold disregard I had for these people, who paid the price for my anger or crossing a line that they may or may not have known was there. The times my fists would do the talking and someone took a beating, much like I used to. I was a hard man, a real badass and felt nothing for what I did and didn't care what my actions would cause in their life. It was never my problem. The code was all that mattered. I felt the fear and physical pain I caused everyone just wash over me. I saw the effects that some of these things had on those people, their families and loved ones and how it haunted them.

I saw the pain that I caused my family and friends. Every misunderstanding and fight. Every time my words had hurt someone. Every time I got angry for no real reason other than I didn't get my way. All of the moments when I ignored my children when all they really wanted was my attention or time. Just a few minutes to show me something or tell me about their day, and I didn't give it to them. The times I got so angry over trivial things and scared them. The times I could've been there for them but wasn't because I had more important things to do. Every time I fought with my wife and caused her pain. The tears she cried over me through the years. This flashed through my head and once again all the pain or hurt slammed into me again and again. I was buried in guilt, shame and fearfulness. I thought this was what my eternity would be. The void. Was this going to be my karma?

I was in the darkness with thoughts of everything that was bad in life running through my head. Like an old record player skipping, going around and around, playing in my head. I had thoughts of all the people I had turned into my victims. People that I knew and people that I never met, whether physically or emotionally, it was very unfair and I was unfair. I can't do this, but this is what I created, this is what I did and what I didn't do. The pain, the suffering and loneliness I created by myself, I needed a second chance to set this right. I cannot stay here it's impossible. It seemed like hours in the darkness, filling the void and hearing the screams, the suffering and cries that still echo in my head till this day. The smell, I could feel it in my throat, it coated my throat and I could taste it, taking my breath away, like eating some rotten food. It could have been seconds or hours, I had no sense of time.

I saw the good I did for others and the stuff I should have done for others. I saw the times I could have helped someone, but chose to walk right by, like they were not there. I saw what I could have done to help someone else or even myself. I could feel it deep down in my soul and the hurt was unbearable. It was a real revelation. I should have done so much, but I was lazy and always wanted the easy way out. I really have not done much in my life that amounted to anything.

Let me just say, when your life is summed up in a review, it doesn't seem like much at all. How life truly changes in a blink of an eye.

I should have done so much more, things I missed the chance to do. I have so much unfinished business. There is no feeling like that in the world, your life is gone and there is not a damn thing that you can do about it. You can't scream "save me" or "I didn't know". There isn't anything you can do. You feel as though you have been cheated, but it was me that cheated me and no one else. I had the chance to do anything, be anyone and the chance to improve the world I lived in, but I choose not to. I choose to sit idly by and let the world pass me. Did my life count for anything at all? I saw Jesus on the cross that flashed right in front of me, like I was there looking up at him, the blood that covered his body was fresh and new.

All of a sudden I felt a warmth rush through my body like a heat wave and a light wash across my face. I was grabbed from the darkness and pulled back. As my fears were washed away by the light, I could see again through the tears that I cried and I could feel the warmth from the bright light warm my body and chase out the cold and clamminess. Fear and the feeling of shame just washed away and were replaced with love and caring.

I was faced with a man that looked like us and his son sat to the right of him. But I knew better, the light that surrounded him, bright and golden, his eyes gentle, ice blue and all knowing, loving, caring. This was God. He said without words, do you know what you did and didn't do? I understood, without a word, I understood completely. I should have made better choices. I should have done more with my life. I should have helped people more. I should have been a better person altogether. I knew what waited for me. God asked if I wanted to stay or return to my family on earth. I was confused, I loved my family, my son Joseph, my daughter Taylor, my wife Carole. I had a good life, but I wanted to stay there with the warmth, the love and understanding. I belonged here and I was finally at peace. Everything was clear in my mind and my heart. For the first time in my whole life I felt a sense of completeness. My mother stepped forward and said, "Joey it isn't your time, you need to go back". I understood, it really wasn't my time and I had a lot more to do on earth. I had to do things right, to put things right in my life and other people's lives. It was time to go back. I was given two amazing gifts, the gift of knowledge and the gift of a second chance at my life. We never seem to understand what a great gift life is while we are living. You never stop to think about losing it, even though, in a blink of an eye, everything you know and have, could change. I was given a second chance and returned to my body like a bolt of lightning.

CHAPTER 9

The Healing Process

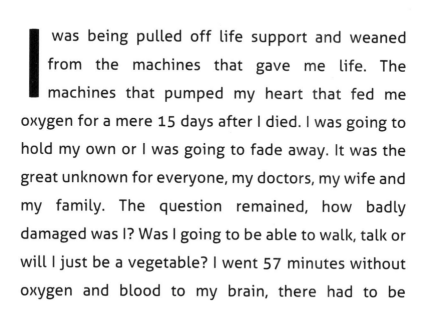

I was being pulled off life support and weaned from the machines that gave me life. The machines that pumped my heart that fed me oxygen for a mere 15 days after I died. I was going to hold my own or I was going to fade away. It was the great unknown for everyone, my doctors, my wife and my family. The question remained, how badly damaged was I? Was I going to be able to walk, talk or will I just be a vegetable? I went 57 minutes without oxygen and blood to my brain, there had to be damage, it was medically impossible to go that long and have things turn out good. There was a rare chance things would be good for me. In cases like this, time is everything and 57 minutes was just way too long. When your heart stops beating, other organs start to stop, like your liver, your brain, your kidneys and everything else. Because your heart sends the signal to shut down, it says we are done and everything starts to shut down. See they just do not bring people back from the dead; there are so many factors, like brain activity, organs working and the quality of life. They might bring back someone that died for a few seconds, or maybe a few minutes, but it's unheard of bringing people back to life after 57 minutes. It's a true act of God and a miracle in every sense of the word. I guess when it's broken down into those words, it's earthshaking and mind-blowing.

It was a funny thing, the nurses that morning, wanted to insert a waste tube in my ass. My wife asked them not to do that, I had family coming and she didn't want them to see me that way. I was getting pulled off life support today anyways. It seemed like the nurses were getting sick of changing my diapers. I think about those now, diapers, really. My wife had something to do and stepped out for a minute. I think maybe a call. When she returned to my room, one nurse said to the other, "Did you tell her?" And my wife said to them "Tell me what"? See Carole is a very strong woman and she protected me through all of this. The nurse told her that they were going to insert the waste tube. Carole said "no way", she said, "maybe when Joey gets pulled off life support and he fails, maybe then would be a good time". The nurses seemed angry with this so Carole called the patient advocate line and they held off from inserting the waste tube. I just think everyone thought that I was going to fail. Just crash and die again.

After being pulled off life support, I could not move my hands or anything, I could barely talk. The nurses put a full-face mask on me for breathing, but no one told the nurses that I could not move my hands and I was basically paralyzed. I got sick and threw up into the mask they put on to help me breathe, I was drowning in my own throw up and there was nothing I could do. Carole walked in and saw what was happening and fought to pull off the mask that was killing me, wow, what a way to finally go I thought to myself. I fought so hard to get here and this one mistake would kill me. How ironic.

I held my own and I started to come out of the fog to everyone's amazement. After waking up, I talked to my wife for a short time and found out what happened. They kept asking me "can you hear me"? Or "can you move this and that"? I could not move my hands or feet, I guess I was locked up, but I could talk and move my eyes. They would ask me if I recognized this person and that person and so on. I had the urge to use the restroom, Carole said, "Oh wait I want to tell the nurses this", and left the room laughing. I was very fragile at that time and the next few days would show them how much damage I had and what the long-term effects could be. The next few days would tell the whole entire story.

When I entered the hospital, my heart ejection fraction was 20, the norm was 55, ejection fraction is a measurement in determining how well your heart is pumping blood and track the damage of the heart (heart failure), and yes, I was very sick man. As my heart started to heal, I was released from the heart center 2 days after being pulled off life support, and on the third day I was transferred to the rehabilitation center in Big Rapids.

I stayed in rehabilitation for one day. I wanted out of there and would do whatever I could to be home in my own bed. The rehabilitation wing was old and outdated and I just didn't want to be there. I had been through a lot and I wanted to be home with my family. My first day in rehab consisted of getting me to do things on my own, like use the bathroom, shower and walking, a lot of walking. As my family came to visit me that night, we sat in the rec/visiting room of the rehabilitation center. One of the nurses that worked on me that fateful night in the ER walked by and asked if I was Joey. I did not recognize her, I said yes and she walked away with tears in her eyes, I thought, wow what did I do wrong to her? The next thing I knew the room was flooded with some of the ER staff that helped me that night. I began to cry, I was so very overwhelmed. Why did I deserve this? These great people that worked on me and gave me their all. I thanked each and every one of them. I met a few nurses that did CPR on me. I met the girl who saved my brain. The list just goes on and on. I still meet people to this day that had a hand, one way or another, in saving my life. It still amazes me how many people truly cared and stepped up that night.

I was supposed to be in physical therapy for at least 2 weeks, after a day, they decided that I could do outpatient, I was healing fast and on the right track to recovery. Plus I was being a pain in the ass asking to be released and go home. I missed being home and in my own bed. I had to assure them I would have someone at home at all times. My family stepped up and filled in. I went home the next day. I was home walking with a walker and sleeping in my own bed for the first time in 18 days. I was pulled off life support 3 days ago, with a slim chance of survival. Today I was home with my family. It's unheard of, it just doesn't medically happen. I felt like the luckiest man alive, I was back home with my family and doing well. But would I take the message I was given and do something with it? Or was it a personal message for me to change my life and correct the wrongs I have done in life? Or would I face the alternative, the blackness, the void, the cries and those screams of the damned? Only time would tell.

I wanted to go and thank the ER team that worked on me and saved my life. As I walked into the hospital upright, I felt a shudder run through my body, this is where it all happened, the good, the bad, me losing my life and gaining it back. They let me back into the ER and as I walked in, I saw people turn and gasp, like they had just seen a ghost. People started to take pictures with me. They wanted some for my memories and some just to have. How do you say thank you to people for saving your life? They are just words and nothing more. But I felt like I owed them the words and more. Because of them, I cheated death, I beat death at its own game, and I was not supposed to be here. However, God saw to it I did indeed stay here. He was with me the night of July 2, 2014.

As I met the rest of the ER team that worked on me that night, out of nowhere here comes this little redheaded nurse, yes the same one I watched working on me from above, like a dream. She said that she climbed on the gurney and was giving me CPR, but I already knew, I had seen her, my vision was right, I did see her, I had goosebumps running down my arms, she was just like I remembered her. I met the ladies and men who worked so hard at saving my life, the whole team of them. I had tears in my eyes and my heart ached, because I just didn't feel worthy when so many people don't get a second chance. I thanked a few nurses and they told me, no thanks needed. They told me this is why we got into the field and that I have given them a reason to keep pushing on. They said they get sick of losing so many, to win a big one like this was awesome. I guess I can understand, but still felt indebted to them.

I finally met Dr. Morris on this visit, my first time meeting the guy who worked so hard and steady on me and never once gave up. He is truly a humble man with a big smile. The reunion was documented and we were both interviewed for the Spectrum Health Website. Being back in that room where I watched myself float above my body was incredibly emotional and chilling. The ER team, Dr. Morris and I, we are family now. These people are great people and I was glad that I had them in my life. I truly believe God puts the right people in your path when you truly need them the most, not just when we want them there. Do I think it was divine intervention? 100 percent YES! There is no other answer, nothing. I started physical therapy and started to walk again, I went to physical therapy for a 30-day run, 3 times a week.

My body was starting to make a comeback, as I started to regain my balance and started to walk on my own, things were getting better. My heart doctors kept a good eye on me the first few months, I had a plumber, (that's what they call the Dr. who does the stents and basically your blood circulation) and I had an electrician, that is the Dr. that takes care of the a-fib, electrical signals to the heart and the flutter. My doctors let me know my heart ejection returned to 55 percent, impossible, right? No, by the grace of God everything is possible.

Things were going so good that I was allowed to start my rehab in the cardiac unit. This is the scariest part of my recovery that I had to face. The rehab unit was going to work me out hard and get my heart back to running right. Every other day I would go to rehab and they would hook me up to a heart monitor, why did they need a heart monitor if you were going to be all right? They informed me they had a crash cart and every one of them was trained to know what to do if I had another heart attack. That didn't bring any comfort to me whatsoever. They said there would be alarms going off if my monitor ever picked up a problem.

I got onto the treadmill and started walking a very slow pace; I was the youngest person here and the slowest. The elderly patients made me look like I was at a snail's speed. I was good with that. The first time I heard the phone ring, I almost stumbled off my treadmill. I thought it was the alarm for my monitor going off. I was scared and I asked if that was me. They just laughed and said I was all right. They must have had someone like me a few times before this. Every time after that, when the phone rang, I would look over and they would shake their head, "it's alright Joey, it's not you". I have to say, I really enjoyed cardiac rehab, the ladies were great and so compassionate to people and their families, they were tough and would push you, but some of the best people I have met.

One day walking out of the hospital, I passed the rehabilitation center I was at for one day, I bumped into the director and he pulled me aside and said, "Joey, do you know how lucky you are?" I told him I kind of get it and he said, "No, you don't get it, less than one percent walk away from what you walked away from, you are a miracle. Enjoy life." He shook my hand and walked down the hall. But I did get it. Every time I stepped outside and felt the sun on my face, every time my granddaughter crawled into my lap and put her head on my shoulder, every time I saw my wife smile at me. Oh boy, did I get it. Yes, I truly was given a second chance in every way, my life, my heart and my organs, all functioned the way they should and I was on the way to recovery.

I was healing physically, but mentally I was a mess. I started to have feelings of guilt, like why was I given a second chance, when a mother of 5 was taken away from her family, that same night in the ER? I felt like she was more important to the world, she had five kids that relied on her to support them. She needed to go to their school games, their marriages, and the birth of her first grandchild and so on. I really felt like

I should have died and was burdened with survivor's guilt. I just felt guilty for surviving. I just did not understand God's plan, I thought I did and how these decisions were made. I started to feel depressed and the night of July 2, 2014 came to haunt me every night, night after night, keeping me up with fear and I could not sleep. I was afraid of dying and that if I closed my eyes, I would never awaken again. I was diagnosed with PTSD and I started to see a counselor. We started to talk a little bit about what I went through and it lead into my childhood memories. As the trust built up between my counselor and me, I started to open up more about what happened and what I felt at night. The reasons why I didn't sleep or was always worried that my heart would fail was survivor's guilt, my survivor's guilt ran deep. I was shown so much and given a second chance. Why me?

Everyone kept telling me "God saved you for a reason because he went way out of his way to do so". You have a purpose in this life and a path to follow. Like I said, I was healing and doing really well for a guy that died for 57 minutes and came back to life. Looking at me from the outside, I was tall, strong looking, I walked without any limp, I didn't talk funny, and I looked like everyone else. You would never imagine what I had been through by the looks of my outer shell. I have been through hell and back, dragged through the mud and I blended well. However, I just fought the fight of my life, I fought for survival, I fought to live another day. I met God! And God was with me the night of July 2, 2014. I am not used to saying that. I am not used to relying on anyone other than myself. I am used to God being a "no show" in my life.

I would have phantom heart pains every now and then. I don't know if it was my mind playing tricks on me or what? I remember one visit to the ER, I was getting checked out and when I was done, I was walking out the door and I heard the one doctor say to the other doctor, "hey, that's that miracle man right there!" Everyone knew who I was. Funny thing what dying does to someone. I started to get stronger with each passing day and I was feeling better than I have felt in years. My memory was a little out of whack, but I was a good actor. I would see people in the store and they would start talking with me like they knew me forever and I could not place the face. If that's the only side effect then I count myself blessed.

CHAPTER 10

The Change

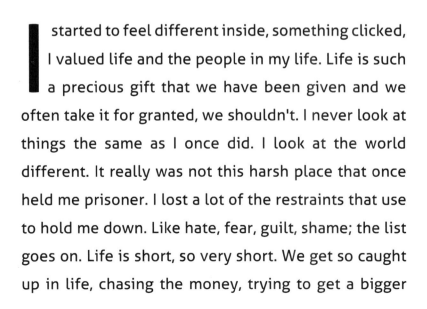

I started to feel different inside, something clicked, I valued life and the people in my life. Life is such a precious gift that we have been given and we often take it for granted, we shouldn't. I never look at things the same as I once did. I look at the world different. It really was not this harsh place that once held me prisoner. I lost a lot of the restraints that use to hold me down. Like hate, fear, guilt, shame; the list goes on. Life is short, so very short. We get so caught up in life, chasing the money, trying to get a bigger house and a better promotion. We forget the little things that make life great and what truly counts. Simple things we take for granted each and every day. Until these things are almost taken away you are faced with what you could have done, what you could have become and the people you should have held a little closer in life.

I felt like a new man, truly reborn again in a big way. I had so much that I held inside me that I never released and I never wanted to face, how do you face your biggest demons? I was ashamed of the abuse I faced as a child that paralyzed me with fear. I was ashamed of the way my mother treated me, physically and mentally. I was ashamed of the words she would throw at me and for so many years I believed I was less than human. Instead of hating her for her abuse physically and mentally, I learned to forgive her. Wow, did I just say that? How do you hate someone for being sick? We are only products of what we are shown. If we are shown hate for so long, we learn to hate, not to love. If we are abused for so long, we become abusers ourselves. Not that we were born as abusers, it's a learned trait. Its real simple, treat people like you want to be treated, all eyes are on us.

After my heart attack I realized the doctors fixed more than my clogged arteries and my a-fib, they fixed a broken heart. A heart that was incapable of feeling things. I now wanted to help other people. Where I used to victimize people, assault people and destroy people's lives, people I didn't even know, I now wanted to change people's lives for the better. What a change on my part, I was healing physically and mentally on both levels. For once I liked the person I was becoming. I was not perfect, but I was good with that, really good with that. I lived my life in the darkness for so long, I didn't know what the light felt like or what doing good felt like. I was a new person inside and out.

We judge so many people from their outward appearance; we are very judgmental people by nature. I have learned not to judge because you never know what this person has been through or is dealing with. Maybe someone is on the edge of suicide, their world is coming to an end and your kind word could pull them back from the edge. Or maybe someone is so lonely and in a dark place, that a kind word might make him or her feel not so alone, loneliness is a terrible feeling. It doesn't matter what our battle is, we all need love, understanding, compassion and a kind word now and again. We need to treat each other differently, not like strangers, but like brothers. I wish when I was 11, someone had a kind word for me, some compassion or a helping hand, but it wasn't there. My life is far from perfect today, I still get confused, I get angry, but I get through. I have been blessed beyond words. I started to make things better for me, like I said, I am not perfect, but I am good enough today and my heart is pure. I am a better person today.

I remembered all the things I saw in the darkness and realized I needed to let go of the negative that I carried inside me all these years, the shame, the anger and the coldness to others. I needed to forgive and I had to forgive. The hardest part of forgiveness was forgiving myself. I single-handedly was my worst enemy. I kept myself a prisoner for so long. I never thought I was good enough for anything, relationships, friends and the list goes on. I don't know if it was the words that echoed in my head. Words that my mother used to say, but it did hold me down and I held myself prisoner in a prison I created. I had to work on me first before I could go any further. I had to face myself, my demons and it wasn't pretty. I was a real hard ass, a tough guy. I took no shit from anyone. I was cold and unfeeling. I had to learn to love all over again as much as I had to learn to walk again. I was damaged and I knew it. Was I damaged beyond fixing?

I started slowing down and actually talking to people. I hated shopping, my ADHD would go crazy in the stores, and I got overloaded fast. I just wanted to always get in and get out as soon as I could, I never wanted to talk with people and I was too busy. As I started to heal, I got to know the kid at the meat counter in Meijer, then everyone knew me and every time I came in, they were like Joey, what's going on? They seemed very happy to see me. I was showing an interest in people that I previously had ignored or treated badly. I felt things starting to stir in my heart and soul.

I remembered what I had been told in the light, how could I ever forget. I had done so much harm to people that didn't deserve it and I needed to make it right. So I begin to do just that, I wanted to help other people going through what I went through. I started to volunteer at the hospital that saved me. I started attending the CPR classes with the good doctor. It seems like anyone that heard my story, in amazement they walked away with tears in their eyes. It's an unbelievable story, I still shake my head in amazement and disbelief. Why was I so lucky to glimpse through heaven's door? What made me deserve this honor? I don't know. I enjoyed doing the classes. If I could make a difference helping these doctors, nurses and physician helpers, that was great. The CPR that was done on me was 100 percent correct and I believe that's why I am alive today. I was making a change for the better.

A few months after I left the hospital, I was asked if I would do a campaign for the hospital that saved my life. A campaign? Me? I am just a humble kid from G town and I have been through the wringer. I said yes and found out that I would be doing a billboard photo shoot. The only photo shoot I had attended before was to get my mug shot taken. They scheduled me an appointment for my photo shoot. As I left that morning, I was nervous, this was all new to me. The whole way to the studio, I just wanted to turn around and go home. I just thought I was not worthy of this, but that was my old self-talking, so I kept going. I made it to the studio. As I got to the studio, I walked in; it was crazy, but all so cool at the same time. I had an assistant; I had a makeup person and a new wardrobe. I went through the motions and got all the pictures done. As nervous as I was, I got it done and I felt good. I felt as though I beat fear that day and I won in a small way. A few months later, I received a call from one of my friends telling me that he just saw me on a billboard in Grand Rapids. I immediately drove to Grand Rapids to check out the billboards for myself. The billboard was huge. There I was making a difference on route 131 in Grand Rapids, Michigan, sharing my story. I had a few billboards around the city. I would later find out from a friend that was flying to Vegas that there were a few at the airport. It was a great experience for me.

I was asked to speak at the good doctor's church one weekend, the parishioners wanted to hear my story. I thought this was a great honor to share my story with his church. I really didn't consider myself a very good speaker, I thought I stumbled over my words and I got nervous. I never talked at a church before. I got asked to leave a church as a kid, but never asked to speak at one. This was all new to me. I was a little nervous on the way to church, on the Sunday I was to speak. Carole and I got there a few minutes early and met the minister. It was a small country church and the people were very nice. The parishioners welcomed me warmly. The pastor wanted to award the doctor with a medal of honor and I thought that was a great idea. After I told my story, Dr. Morris was awarded with a medal of honor after he spoke about his part in the story. Carole and I received one too and it was a great feeling. It was the first time I got a medal of honor. Why were all these good things happening to me? Was it because of the positive changes I am making? God was definitely with me that day. I was in his house. It really felt good.

I was asked to start talking with the cardiac rehab stress classes, now these were my people, heart attack patients. See, when you first come home from having a massive heart attack, it is downright the scariest thing you can go through. You will stay up nights with phantom pains that do not exist, afraid to go to sleep, because you could die in your sleep and never awaken. It is hard to admit that you might be a little vulnerable in a way, because we were strong, healthy people just a short time ago. I enjoyed telling my story and all the cardiac patients could relate. We were a special group and we shared a common bond. I had been where they were now and I came out on the other side.

Livingston County, invited me to speak at a conference about "call times". One of the topics was how and when time of death is called. What factors went into to figuring out when enough time has passed to call time of death on someone and halt resuscitation measures, and what other countries were doing. They had a few doctors from Canada and Mexico. They were anxious to hear my story. This was the largest group of people I have ever had the pleasure of talking to, they were all doctors or in the medical field. I told my story. I talked about my son Joseph having to say goodbye to me at the age of 14 and that the week before the conference, I watched my son graduate from high school and I started to cry. I never thought I would ever have the chance to watch him walk down the aisle to pick up his diploma. My heart melts and emotions clog my throat as I write this, because he has been such a great son. When I could not stand, he would help me stand, when I could not walk, he would help me walk and he always made sure I was safe. He was never once afraid to help me or embarrassed about helping me. He just knew he had to. It was as if he was my protector now and he could not understand how much it meant to me. I was so very blessed to have a son like him and I wish I could thank him a million times a day. Without him, I might not be where I am today or who I am today. I could see other people had tears in their eyes as I walked away from the podium to a standing ovation. I knew they truly understood how lucky of a man I was and what a true miracle this whole deal had been. I felt truly blessed beyond words. Today, I believe God gives me the courage to do the things I fear most.

Chapter 11

The Message in Action

─────── ❧ ❦ ❧ ───────

During my time in the light and the review of my life, I took what I learned and I chose to make some changes. Did I want to continue down the same road I was on and live in the darkness? Or did I want to go back to the light someday? The choice was clear and I understood. I started to apply the changes to my life and to myself. I wanted to feel the sun on my face again and I wanted to be happy, I mean truly happy. It was up to me now to do the right things and treat people the right way. It is hard facing the things we have done or didn't do when things we are ashamed of come into the light. I now believe everything that we do in the dark, will always come to the light, it has to, maybe not this second, but it will. I lived so long in the darkness, could I make the change? It was instilled in me on my visit, that yes, I had to make these changes. It was not a choice, it was burned into my heart, the change was already there, it was there before I entered my body, and I could not reverse even if I wanted to. The awakening and transformation had begun.

God gave me a second chance. Nothing I had seen will ever leave me, not for a second. It is the first thing I think about every morning when I wake up and the last thought I have as I drift off to sleep. It is burned into my memory. I have made many changes in how I treat people around me. My anger towards my mother washed away that day, I had to forgive her and by the time I re-entered my body, I already had. You see, I had a lot of evil stuff happen to me. I always carried it around with me and I would never release it, it was a part of me. I moved on, I moved to another state and put it to the back of my mind, but it was always there, like a bad dream that wakes you up in the night. She was the woman that taught me fear, anger, shame, hate and the list goes on. She gave me her abuse to carry on. For me to carry it all these years, yes, I kept it alive and well. I fed it all these years and made it its own beast. By me carrying that burden, it weighed me down. I just never released it. God gave me the chance to lay it down, release it and no longer give it life. It was dead and no longer had control over my life and me.

That's what I did. No, it's what God did. See, when I came back, I didn't have the baggage anymore; I had forgiven my mother for all the hateful stuff she had done to me. I left it in the past, where it belongs. I hope she is in heaven enjoying the light, the love and I hope the good Lord washed away her pain and suffering.

My mother later in life had a pain pill addiction, I don't know where it started, but she was heavy into the painkillers. Maybe she was trying to leave her own reality, as she knew it. I remember when she died; I got the call from the police back in Massachusetts. I was sad, but I was relieved. She was gone; she could not hurt me anymore. Her suffering was over. I have lost many people in my life and I never shed one tear. I was that empty inside. I did not let anything affect me. I built those walls too high and too strong. When I returned to my body, the walls tumbled down with such force. I now understood what forgiveness was and what sorrow felt like.

I looked at my life and saw how I had turned my inner darkness outwards to others. As a youth, I was damaged so badly. I was devoid of feeling anything and indifferent to other people's feelings. I was a monster not giving a damn about anything but myself. I depended on myself for so long, I truly trusted no one. How could I trust anyone? Everyone that I ever trusted broke my trust, everyone I ever counted on, let me down, everyone that said they would be there, wasn't. It was always me and me alone. I had pushed people away or I treated them how I had been treated as a kid. I was blinded to the truth of the reality of my actions.

I thought back to all the times when I could have said or done something to help someone, I mean words don't cost a penny, but I chose to ignore them and go on my way. I don't know if a kind word would have helped them, but I chose to stay silent. Now, I always have a kind word to say, if it doesn't help the person I am talking to, it helps me and it makes me happy today. Or the times I was indifferent to someone else's pain, it wasn't my problem to understand anyone's pain and suffering, whether I caused it or not. Many times, I was the root of the pain, okay, all of the times, but I was way too blind to see it or ever look at it. I try to be a better person, as I said, I am not perfect, but I am a work in progress and I like the progress, it feels good. I always had turned a blind eye with a cold heart. I thought of all the times I was very selfish, to the people around me, to my friends, my family and even strangers. I could have changed so much if I had my eyes open wide, but instead I chose to go through life with my eyes closed tight. I thank the good Lord for widely opening my eyes, the eyes that once were shut so tight.

I thought about all the times, during my childhood, when one simple word or act of kindness could have made a huge difference, may have put me on a different path. So many child abuse victims have no voice. I want to stand up for them by telling my story. I wanted to help others along their path. I started to look at the lives of others around me. I saw sadness, I felt their pain and I could sense their hurt. I started to look for opportunities to help others; I had to make a difference and give back where I could. I wanted to make that difference, the one I never got. I decided to take that second chance and start doing just that. It was not easy for me, I had caused so much pain, loss and the list goes on. I had to go against everything I knew in my life, I had to relearn how to care about others.

Finally I was ready to reach out to the people I had hurt so deeply in the past. I needed to say I was sorry to so many people, people that I have caused damage to, through my words, my actions and the way I held myself. I had hurt so many people. The word sorry was not in my vocabulary. I was never truly sorry for anything I had ever done but I had all these raw feelings flooding in. I mean saying sorry, they are just words, but now they carried meaning and in my heart, I was truly sorry. I felt remorse. I felt guilt. And I was truly sorry. I began saying sorry to people I hurt in the past and people in my life today. It was both satisfying and truly moving. I released what I held for so long. For so long this negativity had held me back from growing and being a better person.

I had become a monster of sorts and I left a wake of victims in my past. I was good at destroying things, whether relationships, friendships or my family members, I always destroyed something. I was so confused and unclear on how love worked. I always thought love caused you pain, that is what my mother showed us from an early age. I thought love was an evil word that was said to one another. I was broken and I needed to fix myself. I needed to fix my heart and learn to love. I needed to learn to actually love myself before I could truly love anyone. I had to love myself and like the person I had become. That was a hard one.

I got a chance to thank everyone for what he or she had done for me. But there was the one doctor that used to tell my wife, family and I, that things were going to get better. I never had the chance to thank him and tell him how much he was a factor in my recovery. He has no idea what he did for me through all of this.

I received a phone call one day from my good friend Renee. She told me she had a heart attack and was flown to the same heart center where I was a few years earlier. I felt scared but I also felt I was being called to go be with the family and to say my goodbyes. I was at the hospital, preaching my word on heart attacks being the leading cause of death in women. Moreover, this happened to one of my good friends, more like family, than just a friend.

As I was leaving her room after a visit, I was walking down the hall and in disbelief, I see this doctor talking with a group of students. He was showing the students something and once he turned around, I saw his face. This, right here was the doctor I was searching for. I had goosebumps running up my back and chills shooting through my body. I was stunned, I waited a minute to compose myself. I interrupted him and asked him if I looked familiar. I told him my story and I saw a huge smile run across his face. The smile was as if he just cheated the devil in his own game. He said, "Yes, I do remember you now". He then requested me to share my story with his class. I told them my story and through their amazement, they thanked me for sharing my experience. I finally was able to thank the one doctor I didn't have the chance to thank before. I took a picture with him so I could keep that memory with me. See God puts the right people in your path and rewards you for doing well. I really felt cheated with Renee's death. I lost a good friend that day and I will miss her terribly. I know she is in a better place. The good thing is I found the doctor who helped save me with the "thumbs up".

CHAPTER 12

Reflections

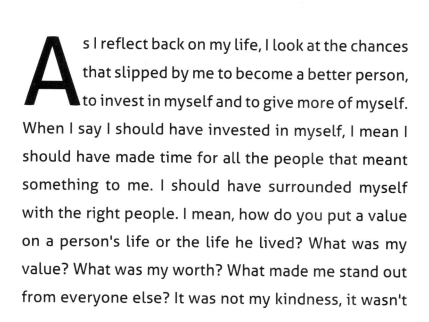

As I reflect back on my life, I look at the chances that slipped by me to become a better person, to invest in myself and to give more of myself. When I say I should have invested in myself, I mean I should have made time for all the people that meant something to me. I should have surrounded myself with the right people. I mean, how do you put a value on a person's life or the life he lived? What was my value? What was my worth? What made me stand out from everyone else? It was not my kindness, it wasn't my helpfulness and it wasn't my sparkling personality. No, it was none of the above. What actually made me different and worthy of saving? I wondered about that a lot in those days and never came up with the right answer. "Why"? "Why me"?

I remember when my mother brought me above my head in the deep part of the ocean and left me there to make it back to shore. How did I make it back to shore? I could not swim, I could not touch the ground and no one was there to help me. Maybe I missed the true person who helped me, keeping me afloat and making sure I did not drown. I never looked at it that way. Through all the abuse I never once died. There were so many times I had come so very close to the edge of death. I know it sounds crazy but maybe I was being protected by something I could not see. Maybe all along, God had a plan for me. After a while I could not feel my mothers' hand hit me anymore. Maybe I was given the gift of numbness through her abuse. Maybe God had something to do with me going out on my own at such a young age. Maybe he knew she was going to hurt me bad so he removed me from that pain that was coming my way or a fate much worse. I was so worried about blaming the good Lord for not shielding me from the abuse, that I never saw him in my life working to save me from a far worse ending, death. God was right there with me and it was hurting him as well to see his child suffering through so much. I never saw him or felt him because my own pain and fear left me too blind.

We just assume that what we are going through at this moment is the most important thing. We assume the world should halt because of what we are going through but the world keeps on spinning, it doesn't stop for a second for you to catch your breath. You have to do the same thing, keep moving with the blows life throws at you, you have a choice, be a soldier and move forward or give up and let it take over your life.

One thing I learned when I was lifted out of my human body, my iPhone was not in my pocket; I could no longer make calls or receive texts. That car of mine that I cherished, I was no longer driving it. The house I paid for, was nowhere in sight. These were earthly belongings and they didn't mean a thing on the other side. They meant absolutely nothing. All those years wasted, thinking people looked up to me, because of what possessions I had.

During my life review I was stripped of everything, I did not see a thing I owned in there. I never saw that I never missed a day on my job or all the money I made, it meant nothing at all. For so many years, I was busy making a life for my family and I. I missed the train altogether, didn't even see it coming. I was too busy, making money for the house, the car, the gadgets; I should have been investing into my family, my kids and their futures. Investing in people doesn't cost a penny. I wasn't invested in the people in my life, maybe the bare minimum and that's not enough. I should have invested into my kids, the same way I invested into my cars, the house and everything else. I should have invested into the world around me, trying to give instead of always taking. There has to be balance. If you want riches in your life, you have to give away all of your riches. If you want to be blessed, you have to give out blessings to others and if you want to be loved, love the world.

I have been surrounded by anger all my life. If the anger were directed at me, I would turn it around and dish it out to everyone else around me. We go through life so angry, so very angry with one another that we never look at the happiness. The things in life that make us happy, the small things that give you a small warm feeling in your heart. Life doesn't need to be complicated, it's quite simple to be honest, we make it complicated and confusing. We live in the dark for so long; we never feel the warmth of the sunlight when it does come out. We are so programmed for negativity and we need to break this chain. I have seen both of the outcomes and trust me; you want to be in the light. Anger, we choose to keep it and hold it like an old friend. We stroke the inferno of rage inside of us, because we get used to it, we look forward to the burn, but we need to let it go. If we don't, it will keep us prisoners forever. Hate does run rampant; it's the devil's number one tool to keep us pinned down. There's so much hate in our world, we need to let it go and learn to love, cause when you are faced with your own life review, you want to go there shining like a new penny, not a penny tarnished from hate. Hate rules our world and we need to eliminate it. Greed, greed is everywhere; we are greedy people today and try to live beyond our means and always want what we cannot have. Like I said, we invest in big houses, big cars and big jobs, but you can't take that with you. What you do take with you, are big hearts, big smiles you earned, and happiness you spread across your world. Today, the real stuff that matters to me are things like a smile from a young person or a grin from an elderly person, those are things that leave you with an uplifted heart.

Our greed takes over every part of our life, how about giving of yourself, giving your time to a soup kitchen, charity and it's not about the money, it's about the giving of oneself. We are all just little parts to a big puzzle. If one part of the puzzle is missing, it will never be complete, never. How about showing a stranger a kind word or a smile? Sometimes something that is so simple could save a life. I just believe God gets our attention in different ways, I was a hard ass, hard head, and he had to hit me a little harder to get my attention. There is nothing to fear in dying, there is fear in living. We worry about something every day- our bills, our car, and our kids. We worry, we get angry and we live wrong. Instead of being angry, try to do something good for someone else. Try to make someone smile. Actually, try to do something good for yourself. Say hello to someone that most people walk past. That one hello you say to a stranger might change or save their life. Kind words don't cost a thing, when it all comes down to it; we are here for such a short time, let's get it right. Make it count. You have to stand up and make a difference; you need to be the message.

When I did good, I did not thank God for being there to help me through, but if something went bad, I was there to blame him for letting me down and not having my back. I never saw the truth, that I let God down and everyone else in my life, I was to blame and no one else. I was so busy blaming other people for my sadness, my failures and my downfalls, I could not see the truth behind the lies, and it's funny how lies cover up a lot of beauty and truth. Lies make it easy to swallow the evil that the devil plants in our hearts. The deception ran deep and true, the only time I talked with God was when I was younger, in trouble and sitting in a jail cell. I would say God help me out of this, I will do the right things and be a changed person, but when I was freed, God slipped to the back of my mind. He was put on the bookshelf, not to be used till next time I had a failure in my life or things got bad. It seems the only time I ever used God's name, was when I was at my lowest. Thinking about it, I always made it through and I was fine to face another day. Was it God making a difference in my life or was

I just lucky? To be honest, I am not that lucky of a person. What if for one second it was divine intervention? It had to be God's hand protecting me. Now that makes more sense.

For a person who didn't believe in God and his existence, I sure talked with him a lot when I was in trouble. Maybe I knew that when I was sitting in that jail cell, cold and alone, he was the only other person in there with me listening, helping keep me company and keeping me sane. I never once thanked him for my beautiful children he gave me, the same children that changed my life and made me a better person. The same children that brought me joy and made me smile with their smiles. The same children that had to say goodbye to me, through the tears in their eyes, while I was on my deathbed. The same children that thought of me as their hero. I should have been there more for them. I should have spent more time at their school plays, their school sports and most of all, when they needed me most. I never gave thanks to God for making sure I made it through the abuse when I was younger. Sure, I dealt with a lot, but I did not die, I might have battle scars, but I am alive. The times I was held under water or left in the deep end, and I made it back to shore. I never gave thanks for making sure I made it through the nights in the burnt out buildings and rat-infested basements in Boston that I used to sleep in. I never gave thanks for helping me make it through DYS as a whole kid, not broken and I never knew what actually kept me together. Serving time in Michigan, in the worst block, in the worst prison with the worst prisoners, where death was every day, I made it through to tell my story, with all the odds stacked against me.

In life, you're going to meet some people or have events that change you in the deepest parts of your soul. There may be that one person or event that takes your shine away and replaces it with darkness. You cannot let it tarnish you to the point of giving in. You have to always look for the silver lining, even in the worst of all events, it's there, trust me, we just need to open our eyes to it. I was locked in a cold cell, under the prison house. I was cold and alone. My cell smelled of body odor and piss from the last prisoner who sat here. Actually, I can say that time of my life was my lowest point. I hit the bottom of the barrel. I wanted to hang myself. I just wanted to be done with all the pain in my heart and the feelings of being alone. I wondered how do I make things better. Well, you dig deep inside of you, get into that survival mode, and start taking little bites, start taking your life back. You can shine like a new penny in a bag of tarnished pennies. It's what you decide to do and what you allow other people to do to you. We are judged by only one being, be accountable.

See, the devil wants us to feel alone and useless. Remember, you are never alone, not even in the darkest of places like the hole under the prison house. It just feels that way and things will get better, they always do. The devil blinds us from the truth, he wants us to fear the unknown, fear death and keep us blinded. We are programmed for negativity at such a young age. If he keeps us blinded, we will never see the truth or the light. Look at the light, never look at the dark, we are God's children and he will never let us fail.

We really need to invest in one another, cause we all get the same size hole when we die, if you're poor, you get the same hole as the rich guy. What counts is our life review, that's where it all counts, learn to give of yourself, your time and instill these values in your children. Teach them the right thing to do and how to treat people. See, our children follow what we show them, if we show them anger, they learn to be angry people, if we show them greed, they are going to be greedy people and if we show them hate, they are going to hate, stronger than we hated, because that is what we taught them. However, if we show them compassion, they will be compassionate people, if we show them love; they will love like they never loved before, if we show them how to give to others, they will give everything they have. First, we need to learn to do this ourselves, you don't want to stand there at judgment day looking at the blackness and wondering how you could have changed it. We need to live each day like we are going to be judged on that day. On July 2, 2014, I never thought that I would be judged that day; I never thought I would die. Surprise, life is so very precious and we take it for granted.

Joseph C Hirl

CHAPTER 13

The Takeaway

used to hear people tell these stories about how they met God, come on, you met God, really?! How they were faced with their own life review. How they entered into a tunnel of light when they died and what they found. Bullshit! I did not believe a single word of it, no way, no chance and they were totally crazy people. See, I was not a believer, whether it was in God, hell or myself. I just thought we lived life, did what we did and were buried in the ground, ticket cashed in. Life is so very short, we made our mark and we moved on. I did not believe in an afterlife or anything close to that. You could talk to me till you were blue in the face, I just did not believe, period! Save that argument for some weak-minded person, who could bend to your beliefs and I that was not that person. I never would be a believer. Nothing was going to change the way I thought, nothing. People in church already get it, the rest of us are missing the big picture. Or we have never been exposed to God or the church life. What is it going to take to make you open your eyes and see the truth, dying of a massive heart attack? I believe God gets our attention in different ways, some people just need an easy reminder, a gentle nudge and then the hard cases like me; we need to be hit with lightning to open our eyes. Well, my eyes are wide open now. I now believe.

My death is different from most, I am so well documented medically, and it's surreal. I just did not wake up on the floor and claim to have had a near death experience; I actually died, completely dead. I made it through a massive heart attack, died for 57 minutes, I was on life support for 15 days, my chances were not good of surviving and it was medically over for me. I have been to heaven and back. I now know why, because God has a bigger plan for me. God wants me to be a messenger. Who is going to make a bigger impact, a little old lady that goes to church every Sunday preaching about the promised land, or a 6'5", tattooed, rough around the edges, ex outlaw biker?

I was the biggest non-believer that you would ever meet, you couldn't tell me there was a God, I just did not believe. How could there be a God in a world of so much pain and suffering, so much loss and confusion. We make this world like it is, not God, we have free will, we choose to hurt one another, we choose to be mean and ugly, we choose to commit crimes against one another. The evil we face every day is manmade and must be handled by man, not some prophet in the Bible. We created this mess and we turn to God to correct every little thing that goes wrong. Sometimes we go through our whole life with our eyes tightly closed, blinded to the truth. So many people want to tear down the belief in God, they have it all wrong and confused, until it's too late. I was that guy! Some people will never accept the truth, even if it hit them square in the face. See the truth is a hard thing to accept. When we live in the dark for so long, it's hard to come out in the light, so very hard.

How do you believe in something that you can't see, or feel, or touch or even understand? It's all so very confusing. How do I make you understand what I have been through and what I have seen? You are going to believe or you will choose not to, it's that simple. You will always have critics, people that will never believe and I am good with that, I almost welcome it, I was that guy, I know the faces of it very well. They spend their whole life doubting everything, eyes closed tightly. That was me, so I completely understand. I don't know if I can change that for anyone through my words, they are only words and how could words comfort you, right? The miracle in life, is saving other human beings, caring and showing love to one another. Now that's the real miracle. I guess I am one of those crazies now, I am very proud to be in this group, this group that has been given a second chance in life. A group that got a rare glimpse behind the curtain of life and sees what waits for all of us. I wish there was a way to record my thoughts, so I could show the world what awaits us. I was the worst of the worst; I was empty and lived day to day. Please don't let this happen to you, you have to change. I'm here today because God has a plan for me. I'm hard headed, but if I can change my life around and become a believer, so can you. We have to; this life is only a stepping-stone.

Am I a miracle or am I just a lucky guy that beat the odds that were stacked against him? Trust me, I am not that lucky of a person; you just read my life story. I went from being dead for 57 minutes, against all odds that I would survive, let alone talk, walk or anything. I have had electricity run through my body so much, I had burn marks on my chest! I was hit with electricity 13 times that night in the ER and another six at the heart center, one time while I was awake.

What are the chances of having a doctor outside on his phone, something he has only done 3 times in his 20-year career? If I was brought through the emergency room, the doctor said I would have for sure died; there would have been not enough time and every second counted. Both Med-flights could not lift off, but by the grace of God I made it to the heart hospital by ambulance, while packed on ice and it was against all odds I would survive. Granted, I had some of the best doctors, nurses and so many others, but God has a plan for me. Why me? I still ask that until this day and will never fully understand. Today, I write my story, I am healed, my heart beats normal and I have been out of a-fib for over a year, Thank God! I have no damage to my heart whatsoever. Now remember, I had four stents put in, I had arteries opened, my heart has had a line burnt across it, twice. The doctors have gone into my heart 4 times through my groin and done repairs. I have been through the wringer and came out on the winning side. My heart is working normally and correct today. I have been blessed in so many ways.

God was there when it really mattered. You can ask any medical person that worked on me, do you think he is a miracle and even the non-believers, say "yes". I wish I could tell you why; I am not too sure myself. I know what I saw, I know what I felt and I know I am here today against all odds. So, am I lucky? No, it is all God's divine plan and I do not question it.

For so many years, I have kept this story to myself, never sharing it with anyone, because I thought these were messages for just me to understand. I was scared how people would treat me; I even questioned myself, was I crazy? If you only knew the courage it takes to come forward and share your story. I had to share it, I didn't have a choice. I could not let one more person die without knowing the truth of what faces them next, just to comfort them in their time of transition. I had to. How do you tell people what you saw and have them understand the depth of it? How do you put into words, all the feelings, the light, so bright and true, the void, the blackness beyond any black I have ever seen? I wanted to keep this message to myself. Then I see so many people dying being afraid, scared, confused, not wanting to let go while fighting for their life and they didn't need to fear a thing. The grief we feel of a loved one's death is a horrible and very painful experience. People who lost loved ones walk around with empty hearts and tear soaked eyes. The loss with no answers as to where do they go and will I ever see them again. I have the answer. Death is surrounded by so much pain, fear of the unknown and not wanting to leave this earthly body. How could I possibly keep this message to myself? I could not be that selfish. The greatest question we have is "what is beyond death's door and what happens when we die"? When you are shown the beauty of heaven, you need to share it and share it with everyone. I may not change the world, but if I can help one person that is suffering right this second, I may change the world for them.

The first message is simple; you have to love each other. Invest in the things that really matter in life- your family, your community, the people you meet every day. Take nobody or nothing for granted. Life can change in an instant, good or bad. It can only take one word, one action, and one choice to make a difference in your life or someone else's. Open your eyes and look around you, really see what is going on. See that single mother struggling to keep herself and her kids fed, see the homeless person on the corner, see that elderly neighbor that lives alone, and see that runaway kid on the street. See the pain in others, and try to make it better, even if it's just a kind word or a smile. You never know what is going on in someone's life. A small investment of time and caring could have a profound impact that you're unaware of. Be kind, be humble and most of all, be human. Live your life in the light. Live your life like someday you will be shown your life in review and be judged by what you do.

I truly believe we are given a life to live and we must first live this life before we are allowed to return home. We are all given a life, whether a minute, a day, a month, a year or 100 years. Some of us are given such a short life, like a baby that passes in birth or right after. Their lifetime was a few hours or maybe more. I believe that baby had served the reason for why they were born. Maybe to show us something or maybe teach us something. Nevertheless, in those few hours, everything has changed for someone. This baby being born affected someone, and its life, even as short as it was had meaning. Some people live until they are over 100 years old; they are very wise and have seen so much in their life. They have had families, seen changes in society, and a million other day-to-day events. How long your time is, you just don't know. No matter how short or long your "Lifetime" is you were brought here to complete your purpose and to return home. Yes, everyone has a lifetime. It's up to you to choose what you do in this lifetime. Whether you change the world or leave it the way it was when you got here. Live every day like your life could end that night. Make a difference, change someone's life, hell, change your own life. Just don't sit by idly and watch the world spin by. See, when your lifetime is over, it's over. You cannot buy more time;

you cannot extend your time on this earth. It is what it is, from start to finish. You are in control of your destiny. Leave a positive footprint in the world and a positive impact on the people of this world. Leave the best memories for your family and friends to remember you by. So when your name is spoken, they have fond memories, not just any memories. Make your life count for something here, make a change, make a difference, but make something.

The second message was not a message for me, well in a way it was, but a message for the world and I would have to share it. Share it with the dying, to comfort them in their hour of death, to reassure them that they are going to a better place and not to fear the guardian angel when he appears, there is nothing to fear. Death is only natural in every way, it just means our "Lifetime" has run its course and it is time to go home.

For those who have lost someone, a husband, a child, a mother or father, it's all right they are going to a better place and yes, heaven does exist. God does exist! I know it's the hardest thing to face, just plain unbearable, but know they are going to be happy and waiting for you. If you are losing a loved one, tell them it's all right to go, tell them you love them and you will see them again and you will be there waiting for them. You have to believe me when I tell you this; you will be reunited with your loved ones that passed before you. Rejoice in their life here on earth; do not take one day for granted. However, don't fear their death either. Understand that they are going to be free, free of pain. Celebrate them leaving their earthly body and going to heaven, to join other loved ones in peace and joy. Please believe me that they will there waiting for you as well.

When it's your time, it's alright to go to the light. It's the way it is supposed to be. Don't fight it, accept it for what it is and allow the beauty to wash over you. When facing death, face it proudly and with dignity, when you cross over, you will be a new person, leaving all your sickness here on earth, you shed that old body and you become a new being, surrounded by love and so much peace. Your earthly pain, suffering, and loneliness will be washed away and replaced with the feeling of joy, understanding and peacefulness. A feeling like no one has ever felt before, it is a type of calmness, understanding and peace like you never could ever imagine.

I am not trying to make death magical by any means; it isn't and never will be. I am just saying it's going to be all right, there is nothing to fear. It's like when the caterpillar turns into the beautiful butterfly, one day he is crawling and the next he is flying, what a beautiful transformation.

Once you cross into the light, that bright overpowering golden light, all earthly restraints fall away. You're free of pain, disease, all of the things that caused you pain and unhappiness. Your loved ones that went before you will welcome you. The light is soft and warm and welcomes you into heaven. You are shown your life and where you fell short. However, you are forgiven if you only believe and accept what God has to show you. If we walk through our life looking at the darkness, we are going to miss all the beautiful things this world has to offer. Death has turned into a dark thing for us, but it shouldn't be. Death should be a celebration of one's life knowing we are going home. Remember, "Life can change in a blink of an eye", when we least expect it. Tell the people around you how much they mean to you and how much you love them; a simple word could change everything.

God Bless.

73679384R00139

Made in the USA
Middletown, DE
16 May 2018